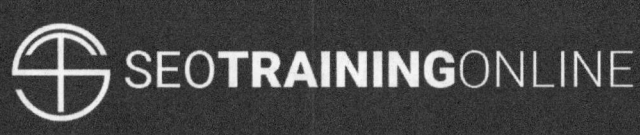

SEO for Recruitment

(CPD Certified)

by SEO Training Online & social:definition

This book can be used on its own or
as a hard-copy companion to the
SEO for Recruitment (CPD Certified) online training course
for those that wish to attain CPD Certification
on completion of their course.

SEO for Recruitment

Published by

seo-training-online.co.uk

email *(for enquiries and orders)*: training@seo-training-online.co.uk

Visit our website, **seo-training-online.co.uk**, for our current online training courses, books and bespoke services.

Copyright © 2024 seo-training-online.co.uk & social:definition

Copyright Notice:

All rights reserved. No part of this publication may be reproduced, stored in a retrieval system, or transmitted in any form or by any means—electronic, mechanical, photocopying, recording, scanning, or otherwise—except as permitted under copyright law or under a license issued by seo-training-online.co.uk or social:definition. Written permission from the publisher is required for any reproduction or transmission.

Permission requests should be addressed to:

seo-training-online.co.uk
c/o Childsdesign,
Devonshire Business Centre,
Works Road,
Letchworth Garden City,
Hertfordshire SG6 1GJ

Or emailed to: **training@seo-training-online.co.uk**

Disclaimer and Limit of Liability:

The publisher, authors, and anyone involved in creating this work make no representations or warranties regarding the accuracy or completeness of its contents. All warranties, including those of fitness for a particular purpose, are expressly disclaimed. No warranties, whether implied or otherwise, are created by sales or promotional materials.

The advice and strategies presented in this book may not be applicable to every situation. This publication is sold with the understanding that the publisher is not providing legal, accounting, or other professional services. If professional advice is required, we recommend consulting a qualified expert or contacting seo-training-online for 1-2-1 consultation.

Neither the publisher nor the authors shall be liable for any damages arising from the use of this book. References to organisations, websites, or other resources do not imply endorsement of their information or recommendations. Please note that websites mentioned in this book may have changed or become unavailable since its publication.

For general information about this book, other books, our training courses and other services, please contact our support team at training@seo-training-online.co.uk or call us within the UK on either 0844 996 0025 or 0844 996 0026 *(code changes may be applicable outside of the UK)*.

About The Authors

seo-training-online.co.uk was born from a need identified by social:definition while working with their clients. Many smaller businesses wanted to manage SEO on their own, seeking straightforward training that would help them advance without the confusion and complexity often introduced by SEO agencies. Larger companies with in-house marketing teams sought more advanced training to bring SEO skills in-house. seo-training-online.co.uk was created to meet these needs—offering a range of training that empowers businesses of all sizes to confidently handle all but the most complex SEO tasks, quickly and easily.

social:definition is a full-service digital agency specialising in online marketing, social media strategy, and SEO. Formed in January 2012, the agency has helped businesses across the UK and globally achieve tangible results from their online marketing efforts. Known for its hands-on approach, social:definition not only provides expert marketing services but also empowers clients by up-skilling them to manage many of their essential tasks in-house. This client-focused philosophy has been instrumental in driving long-term success for businesses, ensuring they can navigate the complexities of digital marketing with confidence and competence.

Graham Childs began his career as a graphic designer in the early to mid-1980s. In 2008, he co-founded his own design agency, childsdesign, with his wife and partner, Lisa. From the start, the agency worked with digital clients and quickly became early adopters of social media. Demonstrating their expertise, the couple gained "Top 250" social brand status with another of their ventures, showing how successful social media marketing can be on a limited budget. Recognising the growing importance of online presence, Graham expanded the agency's services to include website development and SEO, bringing these essential digital marketing capabilities in-house. Graham has also presented seminars on marketing for smaller businesses at a number of shows throughout the UK.

Mick Holloway has a background as a software engineer, which helps with the deep understanding of the technical aspects of SEO, making him a valuable asset in navigating its complexities. Mick first connected with Graham through his business networking venture, 24-7 Business Networking, in 2011, and began collaborating with social:definition in 2012. 24-7 Business Networking goes beyond typical networking—it focuses on providing business owners with insights and training in the digital world. Pre-COVID, Mick successfully grew in-person networking groups across the east of England. Today, he has shifted the focus to online meetings, allowing business owners from anywhere to participate and benefit from his digital expertise.

Lisa Childs began her graphic design career in the early to mid-1980s, with a primary focus on publishing. Over the years, she worked on many prestigious projects, earning numerous industry awards for her exceptional design work. Upon joining childsdesign, Lisa broadened her expertise, leveraging her experience from running a successful blog into managing social media campaigns for clients. She now focuses on creating engaging content and managing social media strategies, helping clients elevate their digital presence with creativity and precision.

SEO for Recruitment

Contents

SEO for Recruitment	1
About The Authors	3
Introduction	17
Overview of the Recruitment Sector	18
Unique SEO Challenges in Recruitment	18
Key SEO Strategies for Recruitment	19
SEO Best Practices for Recruitment	20
Why share *'our'* version of *'SEO for Recruitment'*?	21
The purpose of this course	23

An Introduction to SEO

An Introduction to SEO Learning Objectives	26
The Basics of SEO	26
What is SEO and Why It Is Important?	27
A Brief History of SEO and How It Has Evolved	27
The Difference Between On-Page and Off-Page SEO	27
An Introduction to SEO Test	28
Total Time to Complete An Introduction to SEO	28
The Basics of SEO	29
First – Some definitions	29
Keyword Research	*29*
On-page SEO	*30*
Off-page SEO	*30*
Technical SEO	*31*
Link building	*31*
Further definitions and terms	*31*
What is SEO and Why is it Important?	32
What is SEO and why is it important?	32
Why is it Important?	32
A Brief History of SEO and How it has Evolved	33
The Difference Between On-Page and Off-Page SEO	35

On-Page SEO	35
Off-Page SEO	35
It's Test Time!	**37**

On-Page SEO

On-Page SEO Learning Objectives & Timings	**42**
Introducing On-Page SEO	42
What is On-Page SEO?	42
Why is it Important	42
The Key Components of On-Page SEO	43
On-Page SEO Test	43
Total Time to Complete On-Page SEO	43
Introducing On-Page SEO	**44**
What is On-Page SEO?	**45**
Why is it Important?	**46**
The Key Components of On-Page SEO	**47**
End of Your Second Section – It's Test Time Again!	**50**

Technical SEO

Technical SEO Learning Objectives & Timings	**56**
What is Technical SEO?	56
Technical SEO – Why is it Important?	56
The Key Components of Technical SEO	56
Technical SEO Test	57
Total Time to Complete Technical SEO	57
What is Technical SEO?	**58**
Technical SEO – Why is it Important?	**59**
The Key Components of Technical SEO	**60**
It's Test Time Again!	**62**

Synergy, Myths and Misconceptions

Synergy, Myths and Misconceptions Learning Objectives & Timings	66
The Synergy Between Technical and On-Page SEO	66
Common Misconceptions & Debunk Myths About SEO	66
Clarify Misconceptions	67
Synergy, Myths and Misconceptions Test	67
Total Time to Complete Synergy, Myths and Misconceptions	67
The Synergy Between Technical and On-Page SEO	**68**
Illustrative Example: The Synergy between Technical and On-Page SEO	70
Common Misconceptions & Debunk Myths About SEO	**72**
Debunk myths about SEO	72
SEO Myth: "More Keywords Mean Better SEO"	72
SEO Myth: "SEO Results are Instantaneous"	72
SEO Myth: "SEO is All About Rankings"	73
SEO Myth: "Links are All That Matter in SEO"	73
SEO Myth: "SEO is a One-Time Task"	73
SEO Myth: "Meta Tags are Irrelevant"	74
SEO Myth: "Social Media Doesn't Affect SEO"	74
SEO Myth: "Having a Secure (HTTPS) Website Doesn't Affect SEO"	74
SEO Myth: "Duplicate Content Results in Penalties"	75
SEO Myth: "SEO is Only About Google"	75
SEO Myth: "SEO Can Be Automated Completely"	75
SEO Myth: "More Traffic Equals Better SEO"	76
SEO Myth: "SEO Is Just a Set of Tricks to Manipulate Rankings"	76
SEO Myth: "Image Optimisation Isn't That Important"	76
SEO Myth: "PPC Advertising Improves Organic Rankings"	76
SEO Myth: "SEO Doesn't Apply to Local or Small Businesses"	77
Clarify Misconceptions	**78**
Complexity Over Simplicity:	*78*
Ignoring User Experience:	*78*
Avoiding Technical SEO:	*78*
Time for a Test!	**79**

On-Page SEO Best Practice

On-Page SEO Best Practice Learning Objectives & Timings	84
Introducing On Page SEO Best Practices	84

The Right Numbers and Types of Headers *(h1 – h6)*	84
Proper Keyword Usage and Placement	85
Importance of Title Tags and Meta Descriptions	85
Some Keyword Usage Examples	85
Internal and Outbound Linking	86
Image Optimisation	86
Main Content	87
Content Quality	87
Content Freshness	88
Total Time to Complete On-Page SEO Best Practices	88

Introducing On-Page SEO Best Practices — 89

The Right Numbers and Types of Headers *(h1 – h6)* — 90

Heading Tags Implementation Checklists	90
Headers – General Checklist	*90*
Headers – H1 Tag – Detailed Checklist	*91*
Headers – H2 To H6 Tags – Detailed Checklist	*91*
Additional Tips	92

Proper Keyword Usage and Placement — 93

Keyword Usage and Placement Checklists	94
Keyword Usage And Placement – General Checklist	*94*
Keywords And Title Tag – Detailed Checklist	*95*
Keywords And Meta Description – Detailed Checklist	*95*
Keywords And Headers (H1, H2, H3…) – Detailed Checklist	*95*
Keywords And Body Content – Detailed Checklist	*95*
Keywords And Url – Detailed Checklist	*96*
Additional Tips	96

Importance of Title Tags and Meta Descriptions — 97

Importance of Title Tags and Meta Descriptions Checklists	98
Title Tags – General Checklist	*98*
Meta Description – Generald Checklist	*99*

Some Keyword Usage Examples — 101

Example 1 – Permanent Recruitment	*101*
Example 2 – Freelance Recruitment	*101*
Example 3 – Temp Recruitment	*101*
Example 4 – Executive Recruitment	*102*
Example 5 – IT Recruitment	*102*
Example 6 – Healthcare Recruitment	*103*
Example 7 – Finance Recruitment	*103*
Example 8 – Engineering Recruitment	*103*

Internal and Outbound Linking — 104

Outbound Linking: Extending the Conversation	104
Anchor Text: The Art of Link Labelling	104
Internal and Outbound Linking Checklists	105
Internal Links – General Checklist	*105*
External Links – General Checklist	*106*
Anchor Text – General Checklist	*107*

Image Optimisation — 109

Image Optimisation Checklists	109
Image Optimisation – General Checklist	*109*

Main Content — 111

User Intent: The North Star	111
Structure and Formatting: The Backbone of Clarity	111
Multimedia: The Spice of the Digital World	112
Content Checklists	113
Main Content Optimisation – General Checklist	*113*

Content Quality — 115

Content Quality Checklist	115
Content Quality – General Checklist	*115*

Content Freshness — 118

Content Freshness – General Checklist	*118*

Technical SEO Best Practice

Technical SEO Best Practice Learning Objectives & Timings	**122**
Technical SEO Best Practices Introduction	122
Website Speed	122
Mobile Optimisation	123
Secure Website	123
Accessible Website	123
Schema Markup	124
URL Structure	124
Indexation	125
Total Time to Complete Technical SEO Best Practices	125
Technical SEO Best Practices: Introduction	**126**
The Pillars of Technical Optimisation	126
Website Speed	**128**
Why Speed Matters	128
The Tools and Tricks	128
Optimising for Speed	128

Website Speed Checklist	**129**
Website Speed – General Checklist	*129*
Utilising Google PageSpeed Insights	*129*
Utilising Google Analytics	*129*
Compressing Images	*130*
Website Speed – Specialist Checklist	*130*
Leveraging Browser Caching	*131*
Minimising JavaScript and CSS Files	*131*
Implementing Lazy Loading	*131*
Optimising Server Response Time	*132*
Mobile Performance Optimisation	*132*
Why Mobile Matters	**133**
Responsive Web Design	**133**
Testing and Tweaking	**133**
Mobile Optimisation Checklist	**134**
Mobile Optimisation – General Checklist	*134*
Adopting Responsive Web Design:	*134*
Using Google's Mobile-Friendly Test	*134*
Optimising Images and Media:	*135*
Simplifying Navigation	*135*
Touch-Friendly Design	*136*
Testing on Real Devices	*136*
Core Web Vitals – Largest Contentful Paint **(LCP)**	*136*
Core Web Vitals – First Input Delay **(FID)**	*137*
Core Web Vitals – Cumulative Layout Shift **(CLS)**	*137*
Why HTTPS Matters	**139**
SSL Certificates: Your Website's Shield	*139*
Getting Set Up	*139*
Secure Website Checklist	**140**
Secure Website – General Checklist	*140*
Updating Your Content Management System **(CMS)**	*140*
Updating Plugins and Themes	*140*
Updating Server Software and Scripts	*141*
Obtaining an SSL Certificate	*141*
Installing the SSL Certificate	*142*
Ensuring Complete HTTPS Implementation	*142*
Redirecting HTTP to HTTPS	*142*
Updating Your Site's Settings	*143*
Notifying Search Engines:	*143*
Accessible Website	**144**
Why Accessibility Matters in SEO	**144**
The Technical Roadmap	*144*
Practical and Impactful Changes	*144*
Testing and Compliance	*145*

SEO for Recruitment

Accessible Website Checklist	**146**
Accessible Website – General Checklist	146
Understanding WCAG Levels	146
Use of Alt Text for Images	146
Ensuring Keyboard Navigation	146
Readable and Understandable Content	147
Proper Use of Headings	147
Accessible Forms	148
Use of ARIA (Accessible Rich Internet Applications) Roles	148
Contrast and Colour Considerations	148
Accessible Multimedia	149
Testing and Validation	149
Schema Markup	**150**
Decoding Schema Markup	**150**
The Rich Snippets Advantage	150
Getting Started with Implementation	150
Schema Markup Checklist	**151**
Understanding Schema Markup Implementation – General Checklist	151
Understanding Schema Markup	151
Select The Right Schema Markup – General Checklist	152
Selecting the Right Schema	152
Schema Generation Tools – General Checklist	152
Using Tools for Schema Generation	152
Schema Markup Implementation – General Checklist	153
Implementing Schema Markup	153
Schema Markup Testing – General Checklist	153
Testing Your Implementation	153
Schema Markup Integration – General Checklist	154
CMS Integration	154
SEO Plugins	154
Schema Markup Maintenance – General Checklist	154
Search Console	154
Updates	154
Feedback and Reviews	155
URL Structure	**156**
The Importance of URL Structure	**156**
Keeping It Clear and Descriptive	156
Reflecting Site Hierarchy	156
Avoiding the Pitfalls	157
URL Structure Checklist	**157**
Url Structure – General Checklist	157
Consistency	157
Simplicity	157

Keywords	*157*
Hyphens	*158*
Avoid Special Characters	*158*
Link Checking	*158*
URL Testing	*158*
Creating Concise and Descriptive URLs	*158*
Reflecting Site Hierarchy in URLs	*158*
Keeping URLs Consistent	*159*
Redirecting Old URLs After Changes:	*159*
Using Hyphens to Separate Words:	*159*
Url Structure: Pitfalls To Avoid – General Checklist	*160*
Overuse of Keywords	*160*
Complex and Confusing Structure	*160*
Inconsistent URL Structures	*160*
Using Session IDs in URLs	*161*
Lengthy URLs with Unnecessary Parameters	*161*
Dynamic URLs with Excessive ParametersPitfall:	*161*
Neglecting Case Sensitivity	*162*
Ignoring URL Redirection After Changes	*162*
Use of Robots.txt	**163**
Robots.txt Checklist	**163**
Robots.txt – General Checklist	*163*
Robots.txt	*163*
Set Rules	*164*
Robots.txt Example	*164*
XML Sitemaps	**164**
XML Sitemaps Checklist	**164**
Xml Sitemaps – General Checklist	*164*
Creation	*164*
Sitemap Submission	*165*
Regular Updates	*165*
XML Sitemaps Example	*165*
Canonical Tags	**165**
Canonical Tags Checklist	**165**
Canonical Tags – General Checklist	*165*
Identify Duplicate Content	*165*
Preferred URL's	*166*
Self-referencing tags	*166*
Consistent Use	*166*
Canonical Tags Example	*166*
404 Page and 301 Redirects	**166**
404 Redirects Checklist	**167**
404 And 301 Redirects – General Checklist	*167*
Identify Moved or Deleted Content	*167*
Implement redirects	*167*

404 redirects *167*

Page Experience

Page Experience Learning Objectives & Timings	**170**
Page Experience – Introduction	170
Core Web Vitals	170
Mobile Friendliness	171
Safe Browsing and https	171
Total Time to Complete Page Experience	171
What is Page Experience	172
Why Does Page Experience Matter?	172
Core Web Vitals	**173**
Core Web Vitals Checklist	**174**
Core Web Vitals – General Checklist	*174*
*Largest Contentful Paint **(LCP)***	*174*
*First Input Delay **(FID)***	*175*
*Cumulative Layout Shift **(CLS)***	*175*
Mobile Friendliness	**176**
Mobile Friendliness Checklist	**177**
Mobile Friendliness – General Checklist	*177*
Responsive Design	*177*
Touchscreen Navigation	*177*
Mobile Speed Optimization	*178*
Testing and Refining	*178*
Using Google's Mobile-Friendly Test	*178*
Touch-Friendly Design	*179*
Mobile SEO Considerations	*179*
Safe Browsing and https	**180**
The Importance of a Secure Website	**180**
HTTPS: The Seal of Security	*180*
Why This Matters? SEO and User Trust Go Hand in Hand	*180*
Practical Steps to Enhance Security	*180*
Safe Browsing and HTTPS Checklists	**181**
Safe Browsing – General Checklist	*181*
Monitor for Security Issues	*181*
Implement Security Measures	*182*
Educate Your Users	*182*
Https – General Checklist	*183*
Acquire and Install an SSL/TLS Certificate	*183*
Redirect HTTP to HTTPS	*183*

Updating Your Site's Settings	184
Verify and Test Your HTTPS Setup	184
Notifying Search Engines	184

Key Learning Points and Take-Aways — 186

Key Learning Points and Takeaways	186

How Much Have You Learned? — 188

Test Answers — 198

Introduction to SEO Correct Answers	198
On-Page SEO Correct Answers	198
Technical SEO Correct Answers	198
Synergy, Myths and Misconceptions Correct Answers	198
How Much Have You Learned Correct Answers	198

Glossary

301	200
404	200
A/B Testing	200
Alt Tags	201
Anchor Text	201
Audience	201
Backlinks	201
Black Hat SEO	202
Bounce Rate	202
Brand	202
Canonical Tags	202
Communication	203
Content	203
Content Management System **(CMS)**	**203**
Content Marketing	203
Conversion Funnel	204
Conversion Rates	204
Copywriting	204
CTR	204
Domain Authority	205
Engagement Rate	205
Google Analytics	205
Google Search Console	205
Header Tags	206
Heatmap	206
HTTP	206
HTTPS	207

Indexing	*207*
Internal Links	*207*
IP Address	*207*
Keyword Research	*208*
Keywords	*208*
Landing Page	*208*
Link Building	*209*
Long-Tail Keywords	*209*
Marketing	*209*
Marketing Communication	*209*
Meta Description	*209*
Meta Title	*210*
Mobile Optimisation	*210*
Nofollow Link	*210*
Off-Page SEO	*210*
On-Page SEO	*210*
Organic Traffic	*211*
Outbound Links	*211*
Page Speed	*211*
PPC	*212*
Responsive	*212*
Rich Snippets	*212*
Robots.txt	*213*
Schema	*213*
Search Engines	*213*
Search Intent	*214*
Semantic Search	*214*
*SEO **(search engine optimisation)***	**214**
SERPs	*214*
Social Proof	*215*
SSL	*215*
Technical SEO	*215*
Title Tag	*216*
TSL	*216*
URL	*216*
*User Experience **(UX)***	**216**
User Intent	*217*
White Hat SEO	*217*
XML Sitemap	*217*
Index	**218**

Introduction

Overview of the Recruitment Sector

The recruitment sector is a dynamic and essential part of the job market ecosystem, facilitating connections between job seekers and employers. This sector includes a variety of players such as recruitment agencies, job boards, corporate career pages, and head-hunters. With the digital transformation, most recruitment activities have shifted online, making SEO a critical component for visibility and success.

Unique SEO Challenges in Recruitment

1. **Highly Visual Content:**

   - Recruitment agencies and job boards compete for popular job-related keywords such as "jobs in [city]", "IT jobs", and "marketing careers".
   - Niche industries may face less competition, but still require targeted keyword strategies.

2. **Constantly Updating Content:**

   - Job listings are frequently posted and removed, requiring continuous SEO efforts to keep content fresh and relevant.
   - Regular updates are necessary to maintain high search rankings and attract job seekers.

3. **Balancing Dual Audiences:**

   - Recruitment sites need to cater to both job seekers and employers, creating a need for balanced content that appeals to both groups.
   - Differentiating content strategies to attract candidates while also showcasing services to potential employers can be challenging.

4. **Localised Searches:**

   - Many job searches are geographically specific, necessitating strong local SEO tactics to ensure visibility in regional searches.

Key SEO Strategies for Recruitment

1. Local SEO:

- Optimize for location-based keywords *(e.g., "IT jobs in London")*.
- Create local landing pages for different cities or regions your agency serves.
- Claim and optimize your Google My Business listing to improve local search visibility.

2. Mobile Optimisation:

- Ensure your website is mobile-friendly, as many job seekers use mobile devices to search for jobs.
- Implement responsive design to provide a seamless user experience across all devices.

3. Content Marketing:

- Develop a blog with career advice, industry insights, resume tips, and interview guidance to attract job seekers.
- Create employer-focused content such as hiring guides, industry reports, and case studies to showcase your expertise and attract clients.

4. Schema Markup:

- Use JobPosting schema markup to enhance job listings in search results, increasing visibility and click-through rates.
- Implement Organisation and LocalBusiness schema to improve the visibility of your agency in search results.

5. Backlink Building:

- Build high-quality backlinks from reputable industry sites, blogs, and news outlets.
- Participate in industry forums, webinars, and guest blogging to increase your site's authority.

SEO Best Practices for Recruitment

1. Optimise Job Listings:

   - Use clear, keyword-rich titles and descriptions.
   - Include relevant details such as job location, salary, and benefits.
   - Utilize JobPosting schema markup for enhanced search result visibility.

2. **Leverage Platforms like LinkedIn:**

   - Optimise your profiles, or in LinkedIn (company page) and Facebook (Page), with relevant keywords and detailed descriptions.
   - Post job openings and industry insights regularly to attract followers and improve search visibility.

3. **Create Engaging Content:**

   - Develop a content calendar to regularly publish blogs, articles, and guides.
   - Focus on topics that provide value to both job seekers and employers.
   - Use multimedia content *(videos, infographics)* to increase engagement and shareability.

4. **Technical SEO:**

   - Ensure your website has a fast loading time by optimizing images and leveraging browser caching.
   - Use HTTPS to secure your website and build trust with users.
   - Implement a clear, logical site structure to help search engines index your content efficiently.

SEO is indispensable for recruitment businesses aiming to connect effectively with job seekers and employers. By implementing targeted SEO strategies, such as local SEO, mobile optimization, and content marketing, recruitment agencies can enhance their online presence, attract more qualified candidates, and build stronger relationships with employers. The synergy between technical and on-page SEO efforts is essential for achieving long-term success in the competitive recruitment landscape.

Why share *'our'* version of *'SEO for Recruitment'*?

Here's our version of the omnipresent *'Simple Guide'* to getting the fundamentals of SEO right for your website. This will give you a sound introduction to getting your Website SEO set correctly, and you could use this guide as a template for ongoing future audits.

If you follow these guides, we will call them *'rules'* to give them the significance and importance they deserve, and apply **them all** to your website pages and continue to apply **them all** to future pages you will have implemented about 80% of the total SEO your website needs.

Why are we only sharing 80%? Simply, the Pareto's principle, to get the extra 20% is considerably beyond the scope of this simple guide.

Why do we bother with only a simple guide? Because when consulting, auditing, or mentoring clients *(any of our "Done **with** You" services)* we found ourselves meeting after meeting, repeating, and repeating our advice, the advice you will get in the following pages. A typical cycle would be;

- We audit a website.
- We report on what needs to change.
- We advise, in simple steps, and in micro detail what changes to make.
- We wait 4 weeks and re-audit the website.
- We find the changes have not been applied correctly, or even at all.
- We advise, in micro detail, and in simpler steps what changes to make.
- We wait 4 weeks and re-audit the website.
- We find the changes have not been applied correctly, or even at all.
- We advise, in micro detail, and in simpler steps what changes to make.
- Return to we wait 4 weeks and re-audit the website..

These rules are to aide our clients in understanding our advice, in just how simple the advice is, how direct and how literal the advice is.

How about a couple of examples?

- **"There must only be one H1 tag per page"**. Which literally means, there must be only one H1 tag per page, not two, three or none, etc.

- **"Your TITLE must contain the keyword focus for the page?"**. Which means, the keyword focus for the page MUST appear in the TITLE.

Let us quickly point out *"we are not being, facetious or mean here"*, we often find ourselves three months into a project and still the client has three H1 tags on a page. We have given this a great deal of thought, why do intelligent, high achieving people fail to implement simple instructions, even when its literally *'do this'*?

We think there are a few possible reasons.

- They've been scared off SEO by stories from SEO professionals.
- SEO is perceived as a dark art, complex, complicated, it can't be this simple.
- They have a little knowledge and try to guess why we give such advice and unilaterally try to do more (or less) than we ask.
- Simply overwhelmed.
- Don't believe us and our advice.
- Simply do not want to apply the changes.

There's one more possible reason – they do not believe how important website SEO is, and so subconsciously, don't see the value in what we are asking them to do. If this is you – *EEEEK!* Please believe us, even these basic rules are important in improving the chances of your business success.

Let us know if there are more reasons, please believe us – we are not judging, teasing, or accusing – we would just like to understand why, often, our feedback is not being acted upon. Of course, it is quite OK simply not to want to do any of this SEO stuff, or even not do your own marketing – remember our premium service is a comprehensive *'done for you'* service.

We decided it's also a communications issue, with us failing to impart just how simple the rules are, how important the rules are and how **all** our advice must be applied and **only** our advice. You can see why we are calling them 'rules' not guidelines.

And so here we are, this training course is our attempt to improve our communication and help our clients. Please take it in the spirit intended – we hope this helps. We also welcome, and need, your feedback on how we could make this even easier to understand, because that would inform us how we can make our advice easier to apply.

The purpose of this course

The purpose of this course is to help you understand the basics of SEO, and learn 'how' to let your understanding of SEO inform your digital marketing.

Then, show you how to apply what you have learned. Simple, straightforward tactics:

- Tactics you can prepare for, yourself.
- Research you can do, yourself.
- Results you can understand, yourself.
- Informed decisions *(if you are starting from scratch)* or necessary changes *(if you are working on an existing project or brand)* that you can apply yourself.

And, we are going to show you exactly what to do, every tiny step.

We will focus on teaching you how to do the work that will bring considerable SEO benefits, it's Pareto's law in action. In this course we are getting you to be able to gain maybe 80% of the benefits of SEO, to get you to understand the statistical reports enough to make ongoing, simple, but significant changes to keep your SEO, your content, websites and social media effectiveness.

Shall we start?

An Introduction to SEO

An Introduction to SEO Learning Objectives

This being the first of our learning objective pages, let's introduce you to what to expect. Here's what you'll find on these page:

- **Lesson Overviews:** A brief introduction to each lesson in this section, highlighting key topics and what you will learn.
- **Learning Objectives:** Clear goals for what you will achieve by the end of each lesson, helping you focus on the most important outcomes.
- **Time Management Aids:** To assist in planning your study schedule effectively, we provide an estimated completion time for each lesson. Additionally, for tasks requiring external work—such as research, content creation, or reflective practice—we offer a range from minimum to maximum time you might expect to invest.

This structure is designed to help you maximise your learning efficiency and effectiveness, ensuring you know exactly what's required and can manage your time accordingly.

Here's what you'll find in this section:

The Basics of SEO

Begin your journey into SEO by exploring its fundamental concepts, with no prerequisite knowledge expected.

Timing: 20 minutes

Learning Objectives:

- **Identify the core components of SEO** and understand their role in digital marketing.
- **Recognise the importance of SEO** in enhancing online presence and visibility.
- **Familiarise yourself with SEO terminology** and foundational concepts without needing prior knowledge.

What is SEO and Why It Is Important?

Understand SEO: a crucial tool that amplifies your website's visibility by optimising it for search engine results, ensuring that potential customers can easily find you online.

Timing: 5 minutes

Learning Objectives:

- **Define SEO** and explain its significance in today's digital landscape.
- **Illustrate how SEO can impact a business's online visibility and search engine ranking.**
- **Discuss the role of SEO in driving website traffic** and contributing to business growth.

A Brief History of SEO and How It Has Evolved

Explore the evolution of SEO, tracing its history from simple keyword matching to the sophisticated, algorithm-driven strategies implemented by search engines today.

Timing: 5 minutes

Learning Objectives:

- **Trace the historical development of SEO** from its simple beginnings to its current complexity.
- **Understand the changes in SEO practices** over time due to search engine algorithm updates.
- **Analyse the impact of these changes on SEO strategies** and practices.

The Difference Between On-Page and Off-Page SEO

Distinguishing between on-page tactics, which enhance your own website's visibility, and off-page strategies that build its reputation and authority through external platforms and links..

Timing: 10 minutes

Learning Objectives:

- **Differentiate between on-page and off-page SEO strategies** and understand their unique contributions to SEO.
- **Identify key on-page elements** that can be optimised for improved search engine visibility.
- **Explore off-page techniques** such as link building and social media engagement to enhance site authority and ranking.

An Introduction to SEO Test

Timing: 20 minutes

Total Time to Complete An Introduction to SEO

Total Section Timing: 60 minutes

The Basics of SEO

Welcome to the basics of SEO!

In today's digital age, the world of online content is vast and constantly expanding. As content creators, businesses, and website owners, you have a powerful tool at your disposal to make your online presence stand out and flourish. This tool is known as SEO, and it is the key to unlocking the vast potential of the internet.

But what exactly is SEO, and why is it important?

While we'll dive into the details shortly, it's important to understand that SEO is more than just a buzzword. It's a game-changer that can transform the way your website is found, seen, accessed, and appreciated by your target audience.

In the following sections, we'll embark on a journey to unravel the mysteries of SEO, exploring its significance, benefits, and fundamental principles. It won't be all theoretical and no practical, in fact quite the opposite. Step by step we will briefly explain 'why', and then show you 'how', the emphasis is on the 'how' – as we will equip you with the knowledge needed to optimise your online content and enhance your web presence.

By the end of this module, you will have a good understanding of the basics of SEO and how to apply them to your own website.

First – Some definitions

Keyword Research

In the vast digital landscape, where billions of web pages are vying for attention, understanding how your audience thinks and what they're searching for is nothing short of a superpower. This superpower has a name, it is known as *"Keyword Research."*

Imagine having the ability to anticipate the questions, desires, and needs of your target audience even before they type a single word into a search engine. With effective keyword research, you can gain valuable insights into the phrases and terms your potential visitors use to navigate the internet. Then you use these keywords in your website, blog's... all your content, AND your SEO! This all helps the search engines, and social media platforms serve your content to the people who will be interested in your content.

But keyword research isn't just about 'guessing' what words people might type into a search bar. It's a well-defined process that involves uncovering the words, phrases, and language your target audience are using in their search, and then aligning your content with their search intent.

In the following sections, we'll introduce some keyword research tools, techniques and strategies.

Remember, this is a course on the basics of SEO, so don't be put off – we will clearly show you and guide you through the basic steps you can take to apply keyword research to your SEO efforts, ensuring you are targeting the right keywords.

Keyword research is a huge subject, and if you would like a deeper dive into the world of keyword research, maybe after applying this basic training, we offer a separate courses on keyword research, and content creation (copywriting) where we explore the tools, techniques, and strategies that will empower you to not only rank higher in search results but also create content that truly resonates with your audience.

Get ready to harness the power of keywords and transform your online presence.

On-page SEO

Your website is your digital storefront, and just like a physical store, it needs to be optimised for a great customer experience. On-Page SEO is the toolbox you need to enhance your web pages and make them more attractive to search engines and visitors alike.

In the following sections, we will be diving deeper into the world of On-Page SEO, exploring how to fine-tune your website content, page by page to improve rankings, increase visibility, and ensure your audience finds exactly what they are looking for. It's about making your website both search engine-friendly and user-friendly at the same time, creating a win-win for your online presence.

Off-page SEO

Off-Page SEO is all about what happens away from, or outside of, your website – it's the art of building your site's reputation and authority, enhancing its appeal to both search engines and users globally. Involving strategies and tactics that go beyond your website's borders, such as building quality backlinks, leveraging social media, and mastering the nuances of influencer marketing. These tactics are about establishing your website's authority and trustworthiness in the digital universe.

Technical SEO

Behind every remarkable website, there's a hidden world of Technical SEO. While On-Page SEO focuses on what's visible, Technical SEO works its magic in the background, ensuring your site is fast, reliable, and optimised for search engines.

In the following sections, we'll demystify Technical SEO, delving into the invisible gears and circuits that power your website's performance. From site speed to structured data, we'll cover the technical aspects that can propel your online presence to new heights. Let's embark on the journey to optimise the unseen and enhance your website's functionality.

Link building

In the interconnected web, your website's reputation is often defined by the company it keeps. Link Building is the art of forging connections and building relationships across the internet.

In this section, we'll explore the strategic importance of Link Building in SEO. We'll teach you how to cultivate a network of quality backlinks that not only boost your website's authority but also expand its reach. Get ready to uncover the power of external connections and elevate your online presence through Link Building.

Further definitions and terms

If you have already explored your book, you may have noticed that you may have noticed that we've added further definitions and terms in a section towards the back.

We know that there may be other definitions or terms used throughout this course that you may not fully understand or perhaps are expressed differently by other people or online platforms. So we've included some of the terms used within our course to help you understand how we use them.

OK, let's begin this exciting adventure by understanding the vital role SEO plays in the digital landscape and why it's a crucial skill for anyone looking to succeed online.

What is SEO and Why is it Important?

Just for completeness, let us introduce SEO, this section is a two-minute read if you are new to SEO.

What is SEO and why is it important?

SEO, or Search Engine Optimisation, is the practice of optimising a website to increase its visibility in search engine results for specific keywords. This increased visibility can lead to more visitors and potential customers for a business. SEO is vital in today's digital age because it helps businesses reach their target audience organically, without paying for ads.

Why is it Important?

In a world where most consumers rely on search engines to make informed decisions, appearing on the first page of search engine results can be a game-changer. It helps in:

- **Increasing Visibility:** Optimised websites have a higher chance of getting noticed by potential clients.
- **Enhancing User Experience:** Through organised content structure and responsive design, it ensures a satisfactory user experience.
- **Building Credibility:** Sites that rank higher are often perceived as more credible and authoritative.

A Brief History of SEO and How it has Evolved

SEO is a relatively new field, but it has quickly become one of the most important aspects of online marketing.

The first search engines were developed in the early 1990s, and SEO began to emerge as a distinct field shortly thereafter. At the time, the most important factor in SEO was the number of backlinks that a website had. Backlinks are links from other websites to your own website. The more backlinks that you had, the higher your website would rank in SERPs.

In the late 1990s and early 2000s, search engines began to change their algorithms to focus on other factors in addition to backlinks, such as the quality of a website's content and its relevance to the search terms that users were entering. This change led to several new SEO techniques, such as keyword research and on-page optimisation.

Here is a brief timeline of some of the key milestones in the history of SEO:

- **1991:** The first search engine, Archie, is launched.
- **1993:** Excite is launched and becomes one of the most popular search engines of the time.
- **1994:** AltaVista, Yahoo, and Lycos are launched.
- **1996:** Larry Page and Sergey Brin begin developing Backrub, which would later become Google.
- **1997:** Google is launched.
- **1998:** Google releases its PageRank algorithm, which ranks websites based on the number and quality of their backlinks.
- **1999:** Google's PageRank algorithm becomes the industry standard for ranking websites.
- **2000s:** SEO becomes a major focus for online businesses.
- **2010s:** Google continues to refine its algorithms, and SEO becomes more complex and competitive.
- **2020s:** SEO remains an essential part of any online marketing strategy.

SEO for Recruitment

Today, SEO is a complex and ever-evolving field. Search engines are constantly changing their algorithms, so SEO practitioners need to stay up to date on the latest trends and techniques. However, the basic principles of SEO remain the same: create high-quality, relevant content, research your keywords and let this research inform your optimisation of both your website and your content and build backlinks from other high-quality websites.

- Create high-quality, relevant content.
- Research your keywords and let this research inform your optimisation of both your website and your content,
- Build backlinks from other high-quality websites.

The Difference Between On-Page and Off-Page SEO

Let us learn more about the two primary 'branches' of SEO, on-page, and off-page. Two sides of the same coin that is search engine optimisation, each addressing different aspects of website optimisation to improve search rankings and visibility.

On-Page SEO

This is the process of optimising various elements on your website itself. It includes technical aspects like site speed and mobile responsiveness, as well as content-related aspects like keyword optimisation, the use of headers, meta tags, and image alt texts.

On-page SEO is about making your site as accessible and understandable as possible to search engines. It's a meticulous process of ensuring each web page is structured and presented in a way that search engines can easily interpret and users can seamlessly navigate. This includes optimising your content for relevant keywords to improve its relevancy to search queries, structuring your HTML to highlight important content, and ensuring your website's overall performance is top-notch.

A well-optimised page not only ranks higher but also provides a better user experience, leading to increased engagement and potentially higher conversion rates.

Off-Page SEO

In contrast, off-page SEO encompasses actions taken outside of your website to impact your rankings within search engine results pages *(SERPs)*. This primarily involves building backlinks, which are links from other websites to yours.

Backlinks from reputable and relevant sites act as endorsements, signalling to search engines that your content is valuable and trustworthy. However, off-page SEO is more than just backlink building; it also includes strategies like social media marketing, influencer collaborations, guest blogging, and more. These activities help increase your website's exposure and authority, contributing to its overall reputation in the digital ecosystem.

SEO for Recruitment

Off-page SEO is, in essence, about cultivating a strong, positive presence for your website in the broader online community. It's akin to building your site's reputation, where external sources vouch for your content's quality and relevance.

The synergy of on-page and off-page SEO strategies is crucial for a successful SEO campaign. While on-page SEO ensures that your website is optimised and ready to be ranked, off-page SEO builds the authority and trust that persuade search engines to place your site higher in their rankings. Together, they create a holistic approach that not only draws visitors to your site but also encourages other sites and users to recommend and link to your content.

It's Test Time!

You've reach the end of your first section *'An introduction to SEO'*.

Before you mark this complete we'd like to give you a quick test.

Here are just eight questions to test your understanding of SEO so far, and how important it is to your business.

Once you've answered all of the questions you'll find the answers towards the back of this book.

To test yourself. Give yourself 20 minutes to complete.

We're suggesting that if you don't get 75% of the questions correct *(that's 6 out of 8)* that you think again about what you've learned so far before moving on to understand the value SEO brings to your marketing efforts.

1. What is SEO?

    A) A type of online advertising.

    B) A process for increasing a website's visibility in search engines.

    C) A tool for email marketing.

    D) A coding language for website development.

Your Answer:

___

2. Why is keyword research considered a superpower in the context of SEO?

    A) It allows you to predict future market trends.

    B) It helps understand what your audience is searching for online.

    C) It makes your website load faster.

    D) It protects your content from plagiarism

Your Answer:

___

SEO for Recruitment

3. **What is the primary focus of On-Page SEO?**

    A) Building a website's social media presence.

    B) Optimising elements within the website for better search engine visibility.

    C) Acquiring backlinks from other websites.

    D) Promoting content through influencers.

Your Answer:

4. **Which of the following is a key component of Off-Page SEO?**

    A) Optimising website HTML structure.

    B) Improving website load times.

    C) Acquiring high-quality backlinks from other sites.

    D) Using relevant keywords in website content.

Your Answer:

5. **What is the primary purpose of Technical SEO?**

    A) To write content that goes viral on social media.

    B) To optimise the infrastructure of a website for better indexing and crawling by search engines.

    C) To create advertisements for search engines.

    D) To collect emails for marketing.

Your Answer:

SEO for Recruitment

6. **How does On-Page SEO improve a user's experience on a website?**

    A) By increasing the website's exposure on social media.

    B) By structuring the website to make it easy to navigate and understand.

    C) By collaborating with influencers to enhance content.

    D) By engaging in guest blogging.

Your Answer:

7. **What role does Off-Page SEO play in improving a website's SEO?**

    A) It involves editing the website's backend coding only.

    B) It focuses on building internal link structures within the site.

    C) It includes activities like link building and social media engagement.

    D) It is concerned with the visual design of the website.

Your Answer:

8. **Why is the synergy of On-Page and Off-Page SEO crucial for a successful SEO campaign?**

    A) It ensures that both social media and search engines are fully leveraged.

    B) It combines site optimisation with external marketing to enhance site credibility and rankings.

    C) It keeps the website secure against cyber threats.

    D) It reduces the cost of advertising on search engines.

Your Answer:

On-Page SEO

On-Page SEO Learning Objectives & Timings

Introducing On-Page SEO

Step into the world of On-Page SEO, where we optimise individual web pages to rank higher and earn more relevant traffic in search engines through methodical strategies and deliberate content creation.

Timing: 2 minutes

Learning Objectives:

- **Understand the role of On-Page SEO** in improving website rankings and increasing relevant traffic.
- **Appreciate the immediate impact of applied On-Page SEO techniques** on the visibility of a web page.

What is On-Page SEO?

On-page SEO involves optimising individual web pages for specific keywords to secure higher rankings and garner more relevant traffic from search engines, all by refining both the content and HTML source code.

Timing: 2 minutes

Learning Objectives:

- **Define On-Page SEO** and differentiate it from other forms of SEO.

Why is it Important

On-page SEO is vital. It helps search engines understand your website and its content, as well as identify whether it is relevant to a searcher's query, improving your visibility and driving more targeted traffic.

Timing: 2 minutes

SEO for Recruitment

Learning Objectives:

- **Explain the significance of On-Page SEO** in search engines' understanding and ranking of web pages.

- **Illustrate how On-Page SEO enhances a website's relevance** and authority for specific search queries.

- **Discuss the role of On-Page SEO in improving user experience** and engagement on a website.

The Key Components of On-Page SEO

Explore the key components of On-Page SEO, from crafting compelling content and utilising keywords effectively, to optimising images and ensuring that your website is easily navigable, all with the aim to enhance your site's visibility in search engine results.

Timing: 5 minutes

Learning Objectives:

- **Explore the essential components of On-Page SEO**, such as title tags, headers, meta descriptions, and keyword optimisation.

- **Learn how to effectively craft content** that is both engaging for users and optimised for search engines.

- **Understand the technical aspects of On-Page SEO**, including image optimisation, URL structure, and internal linking.

On-Page SEO Test

Timing: 20 minutes

Total Time to Complete On-Page SEO

Total Section Timing: 49 minutes

Introducing On-Page SEO

In today's fast-paced digital world, it's vital for businesses to stand out online. **'On-Page SEO' is a strategic tool** that can help your website get noticed amidst a sea of online platforms.

So, we know On-Page SEO refers to the process of optimising various front-end and content elements of your web pages to make them more search engine friendly.

By optimising these factors, you can help search engines understand the context and content of your pages, which can lead to higher rankings in search engine results pages *(SERPs)* and increased organic traffic.

What is On-Page SEO?

At its core, *"On-Page SEO"*, short for *"On-Page Search Engine Optimisation"*, involves all the strategies implemented directly on your website to improve its visibility and ranking on search engine results pages *(SERPs)* and earning more relevant traffic.

In simple terms, it's about making your website *'search engine friendly'*, which helps in attracting more viewers or customers to your site.

Why is it Important?

Mastering the art of on-page SEO is pivotal in the digital landscape, where the competition for online visibility is fierce and ever-growing. This facet of SEO is all about refining and optimising the elements within your website to make it more appealing and accessible to both search engines and users.

Let's explore why on-page SEO is not just beneficial, but essential for any successful online presence.

- **Improves Search Engine Rankings:**
  Properly optimised pages are more easily understood by search engines, which can lead to higher rankings.

- **Enhances User Experience:**
  On-page SEO isn't just about pleasing search engines. It's also about providing a better user experience. Well-optimised pages load faster, are more navigable, and provide clearer information, which can help keep visitors on your site longer and reduce bounce rates.

- **Increases Organic Traffic:**
  Higher rankings in search results lead to more visibility, which in turn can increase the number of visitors to your site through organic search.

- **Boosts Conversion Rates:**
  By aligning page content with user intent, on-page SEO helps attract more relevant traffic, which can lead to higher conversion rates.

- **Supports Content Marketing Efforts:**
  On-page SEO helps ensure that your content marketing efforts pay off, as even the best content needs proper SEO to be found and appreciated by your target audience.

The Key Components of On-Page SEO

Grasping the key components of on-page SEO is akin to mastering the ingredients of a winning recipe in the digital marketing kitchen. Each element, from keyword optimisation to technical SEO, plays a distinct and crucial role in enhancing your website's visibility and appeal to both search engines and users.

We introduce these components now, because, while we will lead you by the hand applying a checklist of tactics; when working on one tactic, or component, you need to bear in mind other components. SEO needs a holistic approach; it's about comprehensively integrating the components to create a harmonious and effective online presence. To do that, we need to know what these components are.

This knowledge empowers you to craft web pages that not only rank well but also deliver a superior user experience, driving both traffic and engagement. Let's delve into these key components to unveil how each contributes to the overarching goal of a successful and impactful website.

Simply put, understanding the key components of On-Page SEO can provide a strategic edge. Here are some pivotal elements:

- **Keyword Optimisation:**
  This involves strategically integrating relevant keywords within your content, including in the URL, title, headers, meta tags, and throughout the body text. The key is to use them naturally and avoid overstuffing.

- **Content Quality:**
  High-quality, informative, and original content is crucial. It should provide value to your audience, meet their search intent, and be structured and written in a way that's easy to read and understand.

- **Meta Descriptions:**
  This is a brief description of a page that appears under the title in search results. While it doesn't directly influence rankings, a well-crafted meta description can improve click-through rates by providing a clear and enticing summary of the page's content and therefore encourage users to click through to your website.

- **Title Tags:**
  The title tag, which appears in the browser tab and in search results, is a primary HTML element that indicates the topic of a page. It should be concise, include

target keywords, and be compelling enough to encourage clicks from search results.

- **Header Tags** *(H1, H2, etc.)*:
Headers help structure the content, making it easier for both users and search engines to read and understand. The H1 tag is typically the main title of your page and should include the primary keyword. Subsequent headers *(H2, H3, etc.)* are used for subheadings and should be used in a hierarchical manner.

- **Image Optimisation:**
This includes using descriptive file names and *'alt'* text for images. This not only helps search engines understand the images but also improves accessibility for users with screen readers. Additionally, optimising image file sizes helps improve page load speeds.

- **URL Structure:**
URLs should be clear, concise, and descriptive, ideally containing the target keyword. A well-structured URL helps users and search engines understand what the page is about.

- **Mobile-Friendliness:**
Mobile friendliness is a critical component of on-page SEO as it directly impacts a website's usability and search engine rankings, especially with the prevalence of mobile browsing. Google's mobile-first indexing approach prioritises mobile-optimised sites, making mobile friendliness essential for achieving higher rankings. Additionally, a mobile-friendly website enhances user experience, significantly influencing factors like dwell time and bounce rate, which are important for SEO.

- **Internal Linking:**
Strategically linking to other relevant pages within your site helps search engines crawl your site more effectively and can keep users engaged with your content longer, which enhances the user experience and can potentially improve your site's SEO.

- **Technical SEO:**
Technical SEO pertains to the optimisation of your website's infrastructure to ensure that search engines can crawl and index its content effectively. In this document we will dive much deeper into Technical SEO. More on this later.

As we move forward in using digital platforms to grow our business, putting On-Page SEO strategies to work can be a key driver of our success. Though it may take time to fully grasp all its nuances, attention to detail and being strategic can lead to great results.

On-page SEO is a blend of technical finesse and content excellence, ensuring that every aspect of your website contributes positively to its overall search performance. We'll help you use On-Page, and Technical SEO not just to be seen, but to build a strong and trustworthy online reputation based on quality and user satisfaction.

End of Your Second Section – It's Test Time Again!

So, you've reach the end of your courses second section *'On-Page SEO'*.

We're inviting you to take another short test.

You may be asking yourself, *'why another test?'*. Well, let's take you back to our introduction. We've worked with a lot of different people and we know that some just skim through the training just wanting to get to what they think is *'the good stuff'* without understanding the foundations. In our experience, understanding the foundations makes *'the good stuff'* even better, and, easier.

So don't cheat yourself, see how much you've taken in and understood, as understanding the principles now, will make it simpler further down the line.

Once you've answered all of the questions you'll find the answers towards the back of this book.

To test yourself, again, give yourself 20 minutes to complete.

As before, we're suggesting that if you don't get 75% of the questions correct *(that's 6 out of 8)* that you think again about what you've learned so far before moving on to understand the value SEO brings to your marketing efforts.

1. What is the primary goal of on-page SEO?

    A) To obtain external backlinks.

    B) To optimise internal content and structure for search engines.

    C) To engage with customers on social media.

    D) To increase pay-per-click advertising.

Your Answer:

SEO for Recruitment

2. Which of the following is NOT a benefit of on-page SEO?

   A) Improved search engine rankings.

   B) Increased external backlinks.

   C) Higher conversion rates.

   D) Enhanced user experience.

Your Answer:

3. What role do meta descriptions play in on-page SEO?

   A) Directly influence search engine rankings.

   B) Improve click-through rates from search results.

   C) Increase the number of backlinks to the page.

   D) Optimise the website for mobile devices.

Your Answer:

4. How does optimising header tags benefit a website?

   A) They increase the website's loading speed.

   B) They organise content into a clear, readable structure for users and search engines.

   C) They automatically improve the site's security.

   D) They generate external backlinks.

Your Answer:

SEO for Recruitment

5. What is a critical component of making a website mobile-friendly?

    A) Creating compelling meta descriptions.

    B) Building a complex URL structure.

    C) Optimising the site for mobile devices.

    D) Using high-resolution images only.

Your Answer:
_____

6. Why is keyword optimisation crucial for on-page SEO?

    A) It increases the website's security against cyber threats.

    B) It ensures that content is aligned with what users are searching for, improving relevance and visibility.

    C) It reduces the overall cost of maintaining the website.

    D) It automatically increases the website's speed and performance.

Your Answer:
_____

7. Which element of on-page SEO is primarily responsible for improving the structure and readability of content on a web page?

    A) Internal linking.

    B) Meta descriptions.

    C) Image optimisation.

    D) Header tags (H1, H2, etc.).

Your Answer:
_____

8. How does internal linking benefit a website's on-page SEO?

A) It directly increases the site's visibility on social media platforms.

B) It helps search engines understand the site structure and improves user navigation across the site.

C) It decreases the website's load time by reducing image sizes.

D) It enhances the security of the website's data.

Your Answer:

Technical SEO

Technical SEO Learning Objectives & Timings

What is Technical SEO?

Behind-the-scenes elements of optimisation, focusing on improving website infrastructure, enhancing crawlability, and ensuring that search engines can accurately index website content to augment visibility and usability.

Timing: 2 minutes

Learning Objectives:

- **Define Technical SEO** and explain its role in optimising the infrastructure of websites.
- **Understand how Technical SEO improves a website's crawl-ability** and indexing by search engines.
- **Recognise the impact of Technical SEO** on a site's visibility and usability from a backend perspective.

Technical SEO – Why is it Important?

Technical SEO is fundamental as it ensures that search engines can efficiently access, crawl, and index your website, providing a solid foundation to build your content upon and ensuring users can find and interact with your site seamlessly.

Timing: 5 minutes

Learning Objectives:

- **Illustrate the importance of Technical SEO** in ensuring that search engines can efficiently access and interpret website content.
- **Discuss how Technical SEO forms the foundation** for effective content visibility and user engagement.

The Key Components of Technical SEO

Explore the key components of technical SEO, which encompasses website speed optimisation, mobile-friendliness, secure connections via HTTPS, clear site architecture, and the accurate implementation of robots.txt files, all aimed at enhancing both search engine access and user experience.

Timing: 5 minutes

Learning Objectives:

- **Identify and describe the key components of Technical SEO**, including website speed, mobile responsiveness, and secure connections *(HTTPS)*.

Technical SEO Test

Timing: 20 minutes

Total Time to Complete Technical SEO

Total Section Timing: 32 minutes

What is Technical SEO?

"Technical SEO" refers to the behind-the-scenes actions you can take to optimise the technical aspects of your website to improve your website's ranking on search engine results pages *(SERPs)*.

This includes refining the site architecture, ensuring swift page loading speeds, securing connections, and making the site easy for search engines to crawl, interpret, and index the content of your website. In essence, Technical SEO is about laying a strong, efficient foundation for your website, ensuring it's not just content-rich but also technically sound and user-friendly. It's the groundwork that supports and amplifies all other SEO efforts, from on-page optimisations to content strategy.

Let's delve into what makes Technical SEO indispensable in the digital age and how mastering it can propel your website to new heights in search engine rankings.

Technical SEO – Why is it Important?

Understanding the importance of Technical SEO is key to unlocking the full potential of your website in search engine rankings. It serves as the foundational work that ensures your site is accessible, crawlable, and understandable by search engines. This aspect of SEO is crucial as it directly impacts how search engines index and interpret your site's content.

A technically optimised website not only facilitates better interaction with search bots but also significantly enhances the user experience. Fast loading times, mobile responsiveness, and secure browsing are not just preferred by users; they are now essential ranking factors in search algorithms.

In essence, Technical SEO is not just about meeting technical criteria; it's about providing a smooth, efficient, and safe experience for your users while making sure search engines can seamlessly access and favourably evaluate your site. Neglecting Technical SEO can mean your otherwise valuable content and on-page efforts may not achieve the visibility they deserve.

So, implementing technical SEO is crucial for a few notable reasons:

Improved User Experience:
A well-optimised website offers a smoother and more user-friendly experience, encouraging visitors to spend more time on your site.

Better Rankings:
Search engines reward technically sound websites with higher rankings, increasing your visibility to potential customers.

Mobile Optimisation:
With a significant proportion of online traffic coming from mobile devices, it's essential to have a mobile-optimised website.

The Key Components of Technical SEO

Grasping the key components of Technical SEO is vital for any digital marketer or website owner aiming to excel in the online landscape. Once again, this understanding is not merely about ticking off a checklist; it's about comprehensively optimising your website's technical foundation to ensure maximum visibility and efficiency in search engine results.

Remember:

"SEO needs a holistic approach; it's about comprehensively integrating the components to create a harmonious and effective online presence".

Knowing about these components empowers you to create a website that is not just appealing to your audience but is also structured and coded in a way that search engines can easily navigate and favour. From improving site speed to ensuring mobile-friendliness and secure browsing, each aspect plays a specific and crucial role in enhancing both user experience and search engine ranking. By delving into the depths of Technical SEO, you gain the ability to diagnose and rectify issues that may hinder your website's performance, paving the way for improved visibility, higher traffic, and ultimately, greater success in your online endeavours

To give you a glimpse into what technical SEO entails, here are some of its critical aspects:

Website Speed Optimisation:
Fast loading times are crucial for user engagement and search engine rankings. Slow websites tend to have higher bounce rates and lower average time on page.

Mobile Responsiveness:
With a significant portion of internet traffic coming from mobile devices, a mobile-responsive website is essential for reaching a wider audience and improving search rankings.

SEO for Recruitment

Secure Connections *(HTTPS)*:
HTTPS secures the connection between your website and its visitors, protecting data integrity and confidentiality. It's a trust signal for users and a ranking factor for Google.

Well-Structured URL Architecture:
Clear and logical URLs help users and search engines understand the structure and content of your website, contributing to better user experience and SEO.

Comprehensive XML Sitemap:
An XML sitemap is a file that lists all important pages of your website, making it easier for search engines to crawl and index your content.

Structured Data Markup:
Structured data helps search engines understand the context of your content, enabling rich results in SERPs, which can improve click-through rates.

Consistent Technical Audits:
Regular audits help identify and rectify SEO issues like crawl errors, broken links, and duplicate content, ensuring your website remains optimised for search engines.

It's Test Time Again!

Here once again, are just eight questions to test your understanding of SEO, and how important it is to your business.

Once you've answered all of the questions look to the back of the book to see which questions you answered correctly or incorrectly.

To test yourself, give yourself 20 minutes to complete.

We're suggesting that if you don't get 75% of the questions correct *(6 out of 8)* that you think again about what you've learned so far before moving on to understand the value SEO brings to your marketing efforts.

1. **What is the primary purpose of Technical SEO?**

    A) To increase social media engagement.

    B) To optimise the technical structure of a website for better search engine crawling and indexing.

    C) To create visually appealing content, optimised to load fast and enhance the visitors.

    D) To manage online advertising campaigns.

Your Answer:
___

2. **How does HTTPS improve a website's Technical SEO?**

    A) By speeding up the website's loading time.

    B) By enhancing the visual appeal of the website.

    C) By securing the connection between the website and its visitors, which is a Google ranking factor.

    D) By increasing the number of pages on the website.

Your Answer:
___

3. Why is mobile responsiveness considered crucial in Technical SEO?

   A) It ensures that content is visually appealing on desktops.

   B) It makes a website easier to navigate using a mouse and keyboard.

   C) It optimises a website for better performance on mobile devices, aligning with significant mobile traffic.

   D) It allows for the use of more complex graphics, animations, reels and video's.

Your Answer:

4. What role does a comprehensive XML sitemap play in Technical SEO?

   A) It acts as a visual design element on the website.

   B) It serves as a navigation aid for users to find content easily.

   C) It lists all important pages of a website to aid search engines in crawling and indexing.

   D) It secures the website's data from cyber threats, hackers, ransom ware and denial of service attacks.

Your Answer:

5. Why are regular technical audits important in maintaining Technical SEO?

   A) They help in increasing the website's advertising revenue.

   B) They ensure the website complies, and remains compliant with international laws and changes to internationals laws.

   C) They update the website's design to modern standards .

   D) They identify and rectify SEO issues like crawl errors and broken links to keep the site optimised.

Your Answer:

SEO for Recruitment

6. Which aspect of Technical SEO is directly affected by optimising website speed?

A) Increasing email subscription rates.

B) Reducing bounce rates and improving average time on page.

C) Enhancing the resolution of images on the site.

D) Expanding the website's social media presence.

Your Answer:

7. How does structured data markup benefit a website's Technical SEO?

A) It increases the website's loading speed.

B) It simplifies the website's colour scheme, making it easier to change schemes and themes.

C) It helps search engines understand the content's context, potentially leading to rich results in SERPs.

D) It reduces the amount of text on a webpage.

Your Answer:

8. What is the primary benefit of having a well-structured URL architecture from a Technical SEO perspective?

A) It makes the website look more aesthetically pleasing.

B) It facilitates easier communication via email, structured URL's are easier to remember and less likely to be is-typed.

C) It helps users and search engines understand the structure and content of the website.

D) It allows for more advertisements to be displayed on the website.

Your Answer:

Synergy, Myths and Misconceptions

Synergy, Myths and Misconceptions Learning Objectives & Timings

The Synergy Between Technical and On-Page SEO

Introducing the seamless synergy between technical and on-page SEO, where the foundational and infrastructural optimisations meet content and keyword enhancements, collectively harmonising for a meticulously optimised, user-friendly, and search engine-rewarded website.

Timing: 20 minutes

Learning Objectives:

- **Understand the interconnected roles of Technical and On-Page SEO** in achieving optimal website performance and search engine rankings.
- **Identify specific ways in which technical optimisations support and enhance on-page SEO efforts**, and vice versa.

Common Misconceptions & Debunk Myths About SEO

Addressing prevalent SEO myths, we dissect widespread beliefs to unveil the actualities, providing a clear and accurate framework for your optimization strategies.

Timing: 20 minutes

Learning Objectives:

- **Identify common myths and misconceptions about SEO** that can mislead or deter effective strategy development.
- **Learn the factual underpinnings of SEO practices** to debunk myths and clarify the real impact of various SEO tactics.

- **Cultivate a critical approach to SEO information and strategies** to discern credible insights from widespread SEO myths.

Clarify Misconceptions

Unravel SEO misconceptions, providing a clear view by distinguishing between prevalent misunderstandings and the accurate insights needed for effective search engine optimisation.

Timing: 5 minutes

Learning Objectives:

- **Distinguish between common misconceptions and the truths of SEO**, enhancing the ability to apply effective SEO strategies.
- **Apply accurate SEO knowledge to dispel myths** and adjust strategies accordingly, ensuring alignment with how search engines truly operate.
- **Enhance decision-making in SEO practices** by grounding actions in verified information and rejecting outdated or incorrect assumptions.

Synergy, Myths and Misconceptions Test

Timing: 20 minutes

Total Time to Complete Synergy, Myths and Misconceptions

Total Section Timing: 65 minutes

The Synergy Between Technical and On-Page SEO

In this section, we delve into the intricate interplay between Technical and On-Page SEO, emphasising their combined importance – in a successful SEO strategy there exists a symbiotic relationship between the two:

- Good content *(a focus of on-page SEO)* can only be appreciated and rank well if the website's technical aspects allow it to be accessed quickly and easily *(a focus of technical SEO)*.
- Likewise, even a technically well-optimised website would struggle to rank without high-quality, optimised content.

Technical SEO is a critical part of on-page SEO because it creates a strong foundation upon which to build your content strategy, facilitating improved rankings and a better user experience. Both technical and other on-page SEO strategies must work in harmony to achieve the best results. It is like constructing a building; technical SEO lays the foundation, while the other on-page SEO strategies build the superstructure, creating a stable, and effective presence in the digital space.

This course has an emphasis on the practical application of what you learn. As you learn, and apply, the tactics in this course it's crucial for you to understand that these are not isolated tasks, or one task to be tackled independently. Instead, Technical and On-Page SEO are interdependent facets that, when harmonised, create a more effective and resilient online presence.

Understanding how these two areas complement and strengthen each other is crucial for any comprehensive SEO strategy.

Here are some examples of direct synergies, or correlations, between specific Technical SEO and On-Page SEO elements:

SEO for Recruitment

Page Load Speed and Image Size
(Page Speed Optimisation and Image Optimisation)

- **Direct Correlation:**
  The size of images on a page directly affects the page load speed. Large image files can significantly slow down a website.

- **Synergy:**
  Optimising images *(On-Page SEO)* by compressing file sizes and using appropriate formats directly improves page load speed *(Technical SEO)*, enhancing overall site performance and user experience.

Mobile Responsiveness and Content Layout
(Mobile Optimisation and Content Presentation)

- **Direct Correlation:**
  How content is laid out on a page affects its usability on mobile devices.

- **Synergy:**
  Adapting the content layout *(On-Page SEO)* for smaller screens as part of mobile responsiveness *(Technical SEO)* ensures a better user experience and can improve engagement metrics on mobile devices.

Secure Connections *(HTTPS)* and Conversion Rates
(User Trust and Credibility)

- **Direct Correlation:**
  Users are more likely to trust and complete transactions on secure websites.

- **Synergy:**
  Implementing HTTPS *(Technical SEO)* enhances user trust *(On-Page SEO)*, which can lead to higher conversion rates, particularly for e-commerce and sensitive data transactions.

Structured Data and Rich Snippets
(Structured Data Markup and Content Visibility)

- **Direct Correlation:**
  The use of structured data can influence the appearance of content in search results.

- **Synergy:**
  Applying structured data markup *(Technical SEO)* to content *(On-Page SEO)* can lead to rich snippets in search results, potentially increasing click-through rates.

URL Structure and Keyword Optimisation
(URL Optimisation and Content Relevance)

- **Direct Correlation:**
  The presence of keywords in a URL can reinforce the relevance of content on that page to those keywords.

- **Synergy:**
  Crafting URLs that include relevant keywords *(Technical SEO)* complements on-page keyword optimisation efforts *(On-Page SEO)*, strengthening the overall keyword strategy.

Site Architecture and Internal Linking
(Crawl Efficiency and Content Accessibility)

- **Direct Correlation:**
  A well-organised site structure aids in the efficient crawling of content.

- **Synergy:**
  An intuitive site architecture *(Technical SEO)* paired with strategic internal linking *(On-Page SEO)* not only aids search engines in crawling the site but also helps users navigate and discover more content, improving engagement.

Illustrative Example: The Synergy between Technical and On-Page SEO

Contextual Scenario:

- *Imagine a website, 'recruitmenthub.com', that specializes in offering job search tips and recruitment services. The site has excellent content – informative articles, engaging videos, and a user-friendly layout. However, it's not ranking as well as expected on search engine results pages. This scenario will demonstrate how both Technical and On-Page SEO need to work in harmony for optimal performance.*

Technical SEO Perspective:

- *Upon analysis, it's found that 'recruitmenthub.com' has technical issues: slow loading times due to large image files, a non-responsive design unsuitable for mobile devices, and some pages are not HTTPS secured.*

- These technical shortcomings hinder the website's ability to rank higher, despite having high-quality content. Search engines like Google prioritize user experience, which includes how quickly a page loads and how secure and mobile-friendly a site is.

On-Page SEO Perspective:

- 'recruitmenthub.com' excels in on-page SEO with well-researched articles, effectively used recruitment-related keywords, compelling meta descriptions, and structured content using appropriate header tags.
- However, the impact of this excellent on-page SEO is lessened because the technical aspects of the site create a barrier for search engines to effectively index and rank the site's content.

Synergy and Outcome:

- When 'recruitmenthub.com' addresses its technical issues – optimizing images for faster load times, ensuring mobile responsiveness, and securing pages with HTTPS – the site's technical health improves.
- This improvement in technical SEO complements the site's strong on-page SEO. The high-quality content is now indexed more effectively by search engines, and the enhanced user experience from the technical optimizations leads to better engagement and higher engagement rates (aka lower bounce rates).
- As a result, 'recruitmenthub.com' starts to climb in search rankings, garnering more traffic, and achieving better engagement metrics.

Key Takeaway:

- This example illustrates why a holistic approach to SEO is crucial. Technical SEO creates a strong foundation for a website, enabling it to effectively showcase its on-page optimizations. The interplay between technical proficiency and content excellence is what ultimately drives superior SEO performance. Understanding this synergy helps in crafting strategies that don't just address individual SEO elements in isolation but optimize the website in its entirety for search engines and users alike.

Common Misconceptions & Debunk Myths About SEO

SEO is conceived by many as a dark art. It is far from an exact science; it is a moveable feast and the only constant is there will be change. Let's deal with some myths and misconceptions.

Debunk myths about SEO

SEO Myth: *"More Keywords Mean Better SEO"*

- This is a bit of an old-school thought and, honestly, not the way to go anymore. An old practice was 'Keyword Stuffing' – packing your content full of keywords, these days this will backfire.
- Search engines these days are very clever; they can tell when you're gaming them, and for some years now they have been penalising anyone that's just stuffing keywords in there without offering real value. Instead of shooting up the ranks, you might find your site getting penalised or even ignored by search engines.
- The key? Use keywords carefully, sparingly and in context. Focus on creating content that's useful, engaging, and naturally incorporates your keywords. That's the recipe for SEO success.

SEO Myth: *"SEO Results are Instantaneous"*

- A dangerous myth is that SEO efforts show immediate results. If only it were that easy!
- SEO is more like planting a garden than flipping a switch. You do all the groundwork – picking the right keywords, sprucing up your website, creating awesome content – but then you've got to give it a bit of time to grow and it will require consistent effort and patience encouraging this growth.
- Sometimes you might see a few quick wins, which is great, but the real magic of SEO happens over the long haul. It can take several months to really start seeing the fruits of your labour, like climbing up those search rankings and pulling in more

targeted traffic. It's all about patience and consistent effort. So, think of SEO as a marathon, not a sprint – it's about playing the long game.

SEO Myth: *"SEO is All About Rankings"*

- A common thought, but there's more to the story. Climbing up the Google rankings is a big part of SEO, but it's not the only thing that matters. Think of SEO like preparing for a great party. Getting people to show up is one thing (that's your rankings), but what really counts is what happens once they're there.

- Good SEO is also about making your site a place where visitors want to stick around, have a good time, and find what they need easily. This means focusing on creating a great user experience, having a website that's easy to navigate, and packing it with quality content that's genuinely useful. Because at the end of the day, it's not just about getting visitors; it's about engaging them and maybe even turning them into fans or customers. So while rankings are important, they are not the sole SEO focus.

SEO Myth: *"Links are All That Matter in SEO"*

- While backlinks are really important. They're like votes of confidence from one site to another, and they do play a big part in SEO. But that's not the whole story. Remember our mantra – "SEO needs a holistic approach…". Think of SEO as a jigsaw puzzle, and backlinks are just one piece of the puzzle. So, while backlinks are important, they need to work in harmony with other SEO elements to really make your site shine in search engine rankings.

SEO Myth: *"SEO is a One-Time Task"*

- Many believe that SEO is a set-it-and-forget-it job. Once again, if only it were that simple! In reality, SEO requires ongoing effort, like a garden – it needs regular tending. The online world's always changing search algorithms constantly evolve (like new Google updates!), and so do market trends and user behaviours – plus your competitors keep on optimising.

- Staying on top means regularly updating your content, tweaking your strategy, keeping an eye on what's working (and what's not) – that's how you keep your site growing strong in the search rankings. It's an ongoing journey, not a one-stop destination.

SEO Myth: "Meta Tags are Irrelevant"

- There's something in this one. It is true that meta tags aren't the heavy hitters in SEO they once were, but they've still got a role to play. Think of meta tags as your website's 'elevator pitch' to the search engines and people browsing the web. Your meta description and title tags for example, might not directly lift your rankings, but it's important for catching the eye of someone scrolling through search results as they appear in the Search Results Pages (SERP's).

- A well-crafted meta description can be the difference between someone clicking on your site or passing it by. It's like your webpage's first impression – and we all know how much first impressions count. So, while they might not be the main character in your SEO story, meta tags are definitely supporting characters worth paying attention to.

SEO Myth: "Social Media Doesn't Affect SEO"

- Another very common comment, and while its not entirely wrong, its not as simple as that, quelle surprise – huh?

- So, here's the thing : directly, social media signals (likes and shares) on your social posts are not direct ranking factors, they do not affect your rankings in search results. But, and it's a big but, social media plays an important supporting role. When you are active on social media, sharing great content, engaging with your audience, you're basically spreading the word about your brand. This buzz can drive more traffic to your site as people get curious and click through. Plus, the more your content gets shared around on social media, the more it gets noticed. Sometimes, it might catch the eye of someone who'll link to it from their site – and those backlinks? They're golden for SEO.

- So, while social media signals are not direct ranking factors, social media can significantly impact SEO by driving traffic, increasing brand visibility and recognition, and contributing to the content's authority and backlink profile.

SEO Myth: "Having a Secure (HTTPS) Website Doesn't Affect SEO"

- No, that's a bit off the mark. Let's put it this way – imagine you have two stores, one with a high-tech security system and the other with a flimsy lock on the door. Customers will feel safer in the first, right? It's similar with websites and search engines.

- Google, and others kind of act like these discerning customers. They prefer websites that are secure – that's where HTTPS comes in. It's like a seal of trust. When your site is HTTPS secured, it's telling search engines, 'Hey, I'm safe to visit.' And search engines really value that, it is a ranking factor. Google and other search engines give preference to websites that are secure (HTTPS) over those that are not.

SEO Myth: *"Duplicate Content Results in Penalties"*

- This is a popular myth! Let's clear this up. Think of it like having two very similar shops on a high street. If a customer is looking for something specific, they might get confused about which one to visit. In the world of websites, when you have duplicate content – pages that are really similar or the same – search engines like Google may get confused about which page to show in search results.

- They're not going to penalise you by taking points off your SEO score or anything, it's not about direct penalties, having duplicate content can kind of dilute your visibility in search results, dilute your ranking potential as search engines struggle to determine which content to rank.

- What is true – is that it's always better to have unique, stand-out content on each page.

SEO Myth: *"SEO is Only About Google"*

- Being at the top of Google's search results is awesome, but there's more to SEO than that. It's really about connecting with the right audience and giving them what they need. So, while high rankings are cool, engaging and converting your visitors matters just as much. Also, while Google is the most widely used search engine, optimising for other search engines like Bing, Yahoo, and regional search engines can also drive significant traffic.

SEO Myth: *"SEO Can Be Automated Completely"*

- Well, if only it could be so easy! While some excellent tools that can help make the SEO process more accurate, and more efficient, like tracking your rankings or finding keywords, they are assistants informing us. There's no substitute for the human touch, creativity, empathy and interpretation – especially when it comes to creating engaging content and understanding your audience's needs, their questions, challenges and search intent. SEO tools can help be efficient but not to automate the whole process.

SEO Myth: "More Traffic Equals Better SEO"

- It's easy to think that more traffic is the goal, but what you really want is the right kind of traffic. It's a bit like fishing – it's not just about how many fish you catch, but whether you're catching the right fish. High traffic numbers are great, but they don't tell the whole story. What really matters in SEO is getting the right kind of traffic. You want visitors who are genuinely interested in what you've got, who'll stick around, engage, maybe even convert into customers. Quality over quantity, you know? Attracting visitors who genuinely find your site useful is the real win.

SEO Myth: "SEO Is Just a Set of Tricks to Manipulate Rankings"

- Some people think it's all about cunning tactics to fool search engines (see the article on SEO hats on the social:defintion website). Advice here is simple and direct, good SEO is about making your site better for people who visit it. It's about playing fair and focusing on delivering great content and user experience. Also known as White Hat SEO. Resist gaming the search engines, ignore the 'guru' at your business networking group whose 'cracked' Google...

SEO Myth: "Image Optimisation Isn't That Important"

- Easy one this, it is! Think of images like the spices in a recipe – they might not be the main ingredient, but they totally change the experience. If your images are too large, making your website slow to load not good for both visitors and search engines. But when they're optimised – right size, format, and even tagged correctly – they make your site more appealing and can even give you a little SEO kick. Plus, when people enjoy what they see, they stick around longer, and that's always good for SEO. So, yes, image optimisation is pretty key.

SEO Myth: "PPC Advertising Improves Organic Rankings"

- This is a very common mix-up. PPC (Pay-Per-Click) advertising and organic SEO are two different tools in your toolbox. Paying for ads is like putting up a billboard on a busy street – it gets you noticed quickly. Organic SEO is more like word-of-mouth – building a reputation over time. So, while those ads can quickly definitely get more eyes on your site and can work well alongside your organic efforts, they don't directly boost your organic search rankings. It's like having two separate lanes on the SEO motorway; both heading to the same destination but in their own ways.

SEO Myth: *"SEO Doesn't Apply to Local or Small Businesses"*

- Actually, SEO can be a game-changer for small and local businesses. Think of it like your digital shop window. Just like you'd want your physical shop front to catch the eye of people walking by, SEO helps your online presence catch the eye of folks searching online, especially those local to you. It's about making sure when someone's looking for what you offer in your area, your business pops up. You get to stand out, attract more local customers, and compete against the bigger players. So yes, SEO is definitely not just a big business thing; it's a must-have for businesses of all sizes, especially if you're serving a local community.

Clarify Misconceptions

Complexity Over Simplicity:

- *Often, clients believe SEO strategies have to be complex to be successful, overlooking the power, and results you can get from getting the basic rules in place. Simple, foundational strategies like proper title tags and meta descriptions.*

Ignoring User Experience:

- *Clients might focus intensely on keywords and backlinks while neglecting user experience, not realising that factors like website speed, mobile optimisation, and user-friendly navigation are critical for SEO.*

Avoiding Technical SEO:

- *Some clients shy away from technical SEO, thinking it is too complex or not as important as other aspects. This misconception can lead to overlooked opportunities, as technical SEO, which encompasses aspects like site speed and mobile optimisation, forms the backbone of a successful SEO strategy.*

Time for a Test!

Here are just eight questions to test your understanding of what's true or false when it comes to SEO. Once you've answered all of the questions check and see which questions you answered correctly or incorrectly.

To test yourself, give yourself 20 minutes to complete. We're suggesting that if you don't get 75% of the questions correct *(6 out of 8) you go over this section again* – ideally for this section you'll want to get 100% as it's particularly important to know what's right or wrong here!

1. Why is the synergy between Technical and On-Page SEO crucial for a website's SEO strategy?

    A) It allows for easier website design updates.

    B) Technical SEO creates a strong foundation upon which other on-page SEO strategies can build visibility, rankings and leading to better overall performance.

    C) It reduces the website's dependency on social media.

    D) It focuses only on increasing page views.

Your Answer:

2. What role does HTTPS play in the synergy between Technical and On-Page SEO?

    A) It speeds up the website, reducing load times by compressing video, animations and images.

    B) It enhances user trust and security, which can improve conversion rates and SEO.

    C) It modifies content to be more engaging.

    D) It only affects email deliverability.

Your Answer:

SEO for Recruitment

3. Which synergy example demonstrates the relationship between structured data and content visibility?

    A) Optimising URLs with keywords.

    B) Securing pages with HTTPS to increase user trust.

    C) Enhancing page load speeds through image optimisation.

    D) Using structured data to enable rich snippets in search results.

Your Answer:

---

4. How does optimising site architecture impact Technical and On-Page SEO?

    A) It primarily increases the number of social media followers.

    B) It improves site crawlability and enhances user navigation, benefiting overall SEO.

    C) It changes the website's colour palette and themes to be more SEO-friendly.

    D) It allows for more frequent content updates.

Your Answer:

---

5. Which of the following statements about keyword usage in SEO is true?

    A) More keywords always lead to better SEO performance.

    B) Using keywords sparingly and in context is the most effective approach.

    C) Keyword stuffing is still a popular and effective SEO strategy.

    D) Keywords are no longer relevant in modern SEO practices.

Your Answer:

SEO for Recruitment

6. What is a true statement about the impact of social media on SEO?

A) Social media signals, likes and shares on your social media posts are direct ranking factors in SEO.

B) Social media cannot influence SEO in any way.

C) While not direct ranking factors, social media can enhance SEO through driving traffic, increased visibility and backlinks.

D) Only paid social media advertising affects SEO.

Your Answer:

---

7. What is the impact of PPC advertising on organic SEO rankings?

A) PPC advertising directly improves organic SEO rankings.

B) PPC advertising has no impact on organic SEO but can increase site visibility.

C) PPC advertising reduces organic SEO effectiveness by competing for the same keywords.

D) PPC is a replacement for organic SEO efforts.

Your Answer:

---

8. How does duplicate content affect a website's SEO?

A) Duplicate content leads to immediate and severe penalties from search engines.

B) Search engines may struggle to determine which content to rank, potentially diluting visibility.

C) Duplicate content is favoured by search engines as it indicates thorough coverage of a topic.

D) Duplicate content enhances SEO by allowing the use of more keywords and providing multiple entries in search results.

Your Answer:

On-Page SEO Best Practice

On-Page SEO Best Practice Learning Objectives & Timings

Introducing On Page SEO Best Practices

Understand and implement on-page SEO best practices, focusing on optimising individual pages on your website to ensure they rank higher in search engine results, driving both quality and quantity in web traffic.

Timing: 5 minutes

Learning Objectives:

- **Understand the purpose of on-page SEO** in enhancing individual page visibility.
- **Recognise essential on-page SEO elements** that support search engine ranking.
- **Identify how on-page SEO improves web traffic quality and quantity** for your site.

The Right Numbers and Types of Headers (h1 – h6)

The use of H1-H6 header tags in on-page SEO, learning how to strategically implement these hierarchical elements to structure content effectively, guide search engines, and enhance user experience on your website.

Timing: 30 minutes

Learning Objectives:

- **Understand the role of H1-H6 header tags** in structuring webpage content.
- **Recognise how strategic use of headers** enhances both SEO and user experience.
- **Identify best practices for implementing headers** to guide search engines and improve readability.

Proper Keyword Usage and Placement

Grasp the essentials of proper keyword usage and placement, learning to strategically integrate relevant terms into your content in a manner that is both natural for readers and advantageous for search engine ranking.

Timing: 30 minutes

Learning Objectives:

- **Understand the principles of effective keyword usage** in on-page content.
- **Identify best practices for keyword placement** that enhance search engine visibility.
- **Recognise the importance of natural integration** to balance reader experience with SEO benefits.

Importance of Title Tags and Meta Descriptions

Understand the pivotal role of title tags and meta descriptions in on-page SEO, ensuring that your website's pages not only appeal to users but also communicate relevant, succinct information to search engine algorithms for improved ranking and click-through rates.

Timing: 30 minutes

Learning Objectives:

- **Recognise the role of title tags and meta descriptions** in improving search engine ranking and click-through rates.
- **Understand how these elements communicate page relevance** to both users and search engines.
- **Identify best practices for crafting effective title tags and meta descriptions** that enhance visibility and engagement.

Some Keyword Usage Examples

Examine practical examples of keyword usage in meta data, gaining insights on effectively incorporating relevant keywords into your title tags and meta descriptions to enhance search engine visibility while maintaining user-friendly, engaging content.

Timing: 20 minutes

Learning Objectives:

- **Understand how to incorporate keywords effectively** within title tags and meta descriptions.
- **Analyse practical examples of keyword usage** in meta data to improve search engine visibility.
- **Recognise the balance between keyword relevance and user engagement** for optimised, readable content.

Internal and Outbound Linking

The strategic use of internal and external linking, utilising connections within your website and to external sources to improve navigation, distribute page authority, and enhance user experience while positively influencing SEO.

Timing: 30 minutes

Learning Objectives:

- **Understand the purpose of internal and outbound links** in supporting SEO.
- **Recognise how strategic linking improves website navigation** and user experience.
- **Identify ways that linking distributes page authority** to enhance overall site rankings.

Image Optimisation

The essentials of image optimisation, focusing on reducing load times and ensuring accessibility, while maintaining quality and relevance to provide both superior user experience and additional opportunities for search engine visibility through image search results.

Timing: 30 minutes

Learning Objectives:

- **Understand the role of image optimisation** in enhancing load times and accessibility.

- **Identify best practices for optimising images** without sacrificing quality or relevance.
- **Recognise the impact of optimised images** on user experience and search engine visibility, including image search results.

Main Content

Focus on developing main content that masterfully balances valuable and relevant information for your audience with adherence to SEO best practices, ensuring pages are engaging, informative, and optimized for search engine performance.

Timing: 30 minutes

Learning Objectives:

- **Understand the importance of main content** in delivering value and relevance to your audience.
- **Learn best practices for creating SEO-optimised content** that aligns with search engine criteria.
- **Recognise techniques for balancing audience engagement** with SEO strategies to enhance both readability and search performance.

Content Quality

Focus on developing main content that masterfully balances valuable and relevant information for your audience with adherence to SEO best practices, ensuring pages are engaging, informative, and optimised for search engine performance.

Timing: 30 minutes

Learning Objectives:

- **Understand the role of content quality** in improving both user engagement and SEO ranking.
- **Identify the characteristics of high-quality content**, including relevance, clarity, and accuracy.
- **Learn techniques to align content with SEO best practices**, ensuring it is valuable to readers and optimised for search visibility.

Content Freshness

Understand the significance of keeping your content updated and relevant, as search engines prioritise recent information to provide users with the most accurate and up-to-date search results.

Timing: 30 minutes

Learning Objectives:

- **Recognise the importance of content freshness** in maintaining search engine visibility.
- **Understand how regularly updated content** can improve user engagement and SEO rankings.
- **Learn strategies for keeping content relevant and up-to-date** to meet both user needs and search engine expectations.

Total Time to Complete On-Page SEO Best Practices

Total Section Timing: 265 minutes *(excluding practical integration with your website)*

Introducing On-Page SEO Best Practices

Welcome to the heart of our SEO journey – the *'Best Practices'* section. This is where we transition from theory to action, from learning what SEO is to mastering how to implement it effectively. In the chapters ahead, we will dive into the practical aspects of Basic SEO, equipping you with the knowledge and tools to not just understand but to actively improve your website's search engine performance.

SEO is not just about understanding the rules; it's about applying them in the most effective way. This section is designed to provide you with a hands-on learning experience. We will explore key SEO elements such as headers, keywords, link building, and content strategies – breaking down each component into actionable steps that you can apply directly to your website or project.

Each topic in this section has been carefully selected to cover the foundational aspects of SEO. These are the tried and tested methods that form the cornerstone of any successful SEO strategy. Whether it's perfecting the art of keyword placement, optimising your images for faster page load, or crafting high-quality content that resonates with your audience and search engines, these chapters are your guide to doing SEO the right way.

So, get ready to roll up your sleeves and delve into the world of SEO best practices. With a blend of detailed instructions, practical examples, and interactive exercises, this section is not just about learning; it's about doing. By the end of this journey, you'll not only understand SEO better but also have the skills and confidence to implement what you've learned, elevating your website's search engine ranking and online visibility.

The Right Numbers and Types of Headers (h1 – h6)

Let's talk about headers. We're diving into one of the simplest yet most impactful parts of SEO and web content structure: using headers from H1 to H6. Now, you might be thinking, 'How important can a few headers be?' Well, quite a lot, as it turns out!

Think of headers like the chapter titles and subheadings in a book. They guide the reader *(and search engines)* through your content, breaking it into digestible, easy-to-follow sections. The hierarchy of headers – that is, using H1 for your main title, H2 for major sections, and then H3 to H6 for sub-sections – isn't just about keeping things tidy. It's about crafting a clear, logical path through your content.

But there's a bit more to it. Did you know that headers are also a great place to sprinkle in your keywords? Yes, but the key is to use them naturally. An H1 with your main keyword sets the stage for what your page is about, while H2s and H3s with related keywords reinforce and expand upon your topic.

So, in this section, we'll explore how to use headers effectively understanding and correctly implementing header tags is your first step in on-page SEO best practices. It's not just about SEO; it's about presenting your content in a structured, accessible, and aesthetic manner that is pleasing to your readers.

Rules:

- Have only one H1 tag per page, typically representing the main title or topic.
- Use H2 tags, H3 tags, etc., for subheadings to break down different topics or points within the page logically.
- Incorporate target keywords in your headers, but ensure it reads naturally.

Heading Tags Implementation Checklists

Headers – General Checklist

Single H1 Tag: Use the H1 header for the main title of your page. Like the a book only has one title – make sure there is only one H1 tag used per page to represent the main topic or idea of the content.

- **Example:** If your page is about "Guide to Successful Job Searching," your H1 could be precisely that: Guide to Successful Job Searching.

Logical Hierarchy: Utilise a logical hierarchy of headings *(H1 to H6)* to structure your content efficiently. Use H2 headers for the main sections of your content. Think of these as chapter titles in a book. Use H3, H4, H5, and H6 headers for sub-sections under each H2, getting more specific as you go down the hierarchy.

- **Example:** *For the recruitment guide, H2s could be Understanding the Job Market, Crafting the Perfect Resume, Acing the Interview.*
- **Example:** *Under an H2 like Crafting the Perfect Resume," you might have Resume Formatting Tips, Keywords for Applicant Tracking Systems (ATS), Highlighting Achievements.*

Keyword Incorporation: Keywords should be integrated naturally into your headers. Avoid forcing them or overstuffing.

- **Example:** *If "job search tips" is a keyword, an H2 could be Top Job Search Tips for 2024, naturally incorporating the keyword, and only using it once.*

Headers – H1 Tag – Detailed Checklist

- **Position:** Positioned at the beginning of your content, ideally before any other heading tags.
- **Uniqueness:** Unique for every page and distinctly represents the page content.
- **Descriptive:** Clearly and concisely describes the main topic of the page content.

Headers – H2 To H6 Tags – Detailed Checklist

- **Subtopics and Sections:** Utilised to represent different sections and subtopics in your content.
- **Sequential Use:** Used sequentially without skipping levels, maintaining a clear hierarchy.
- **Descriptive:** Each tag should be descriptive and give a clear indication of the content that follows.

Additional Tips

- **Consistency in Style:** Keep your headers consistent in style and tone throughout the page.

- **Reflecting Content:** Ensure each header accurately reflects the content that follows it. Headers are signposts for readers, guiding them through the text.

- **Engaging and Clear:** Write headers that are both engaging to readers and clear in what the section will cover.

A book analogy is a good one – Book Titles, Chapter Titles and Paragraph Headings always allude to what follows, and what follows always reflects the heading. At least in good books...

Proper Keyword Usage and Placement

Alright, let's get into the nitty-gritty of what often is considered the cornerstone of SEO: Keywords. We've all heard about them, but what are they and but how do you use them the right way?

World's simplest definition of keywords, and just now the definition you need to know. For our basic SEO requirements, we consider keywords as the phrases and words that potential customers type into search engines, that's it, that's all...

And how do 'we' use them? Well, it's not just about throwing a bunch of keywords into your content and hoping for the best. No, it's more like a delicate balancing act – placing the right keywords at the right spots, in the right amount.

First off, you've got to know what your audience is searching for – this is where keyword research comes in. It's like being a detective, uncovering the words and phrases your potential visitors are using. And once you've got this treasure trove of keywords, it's all about using them smartly.

Recognising and utilising the right keywords, the words that your target audience is using in their searching, can bridge the gap between your content and the people who are actively seeking it. By using the words that your target audience is using, you create content that resonates with them. Keywords also help search engines understand the content's subject, making it easier for search engines to serve up your content to relevant search queries. So proper keyword usage and placement can significantly affect where your site ranks in search engine results pages *(SERPs)*.

But here's a crucial thing – avoid going overboard. Stuffing your content with keywords is a big no-no; it can make your content sound unnatural and even get you penalised by search engines. Instead, aim for a natural flow, where your keywords enhance the content, not overpower it.

We'll also look at where to place these keywords. The usual suspects? Your titles, the first paragraph of your content, subheadings – these are prime real estate for your keywords. But remember, it's not just about plastering them everywhere; it's about making them a seamless part of your content.

So, in this section, we'll cover everything from finding the right keywords to weaving them into your content like a pro. Think of it as learning the art of keyword placement, where you strike that perfect balance between SEO optimisation and maintaining the quality and readability of your content. Let's get those keywords working for you, not against you!

Getting keyword usage and placement right is an art that balances SEO needs with delivering a natural, engaging experience for your visitors.

Rules:

- Before using keywords, research to find the most relevant and high-ranking keywords in your niche. Select relevant keywords that your target audience might use to search for your content.

- Incorporate keywords into your content, but **do not** *"stuff"* your content with pointless unnecessary use of the keywords; instead, use them naturally and contextually.

- Incorporate primary keywords in crucial spots: title, meta description, headers, as well as throughout the content.

Keyword Usage and Placement Checklists

Keyword Usage And Placement – General Checklist

Keyword Research: Conduct some keyword research to identify the most relevant and high-performing keywords for your content.

Start by using keyword research tools like Google Keyword Planner, or Ahrefs free tool. Look for keywords relevant to your content that have a decent search volume but not too much competition.

- *Example:* If you're writing about 'job search tips', instead of just targeting 'jobs', look for long-tail keywords like 'tips for job interviews' or 'how to write a CV'.

Keyword Density: Maintain an optimal keyword density, avoid keyword stuffing to prevent penalties from search engines. Aim for a natural flow in your content. A good rule of thumb is to include your primary keyword in about 1-2% of your text. That means 1-2 times per 100 words.

- *Example:* In a 500-word article about 'recruitment strategies', your keyword should appear around 5-10 times, but it should feel natural, not forced.

LSI Keywords: Utilise Latent Semantic Indexing *(LSI)* keywords to help search engines understand the context and relevance of your content.

Keywords And Title Tag – Detailed Checklist

Primary Keyword: Ensure the primary keyword is present in the title tag, preferably near the beginning.

- **Example:** *For a page about "Job Interview Tips," your title tag might start with "Job Interview Tips".*

Relevancy: The title tag should accurately represent the content of the page.

- **Example:** *If your page is a guide, use a title like "Ultimate Guide to Job Interview Tips" instead of something vague like "Interview Advice".*

Length: The title tag length is within the recommended 50-60 characters to display properly in search results.

- **Example:** *Essential Job Interview Tips for Success | RecruitmentHub*

Keywords And Meta Description – Detailed Checklist

Keyword Inclusion: Include the primary keyword naturally within the meta description.

Enticing Description: Write a meta description that is enticing and encourages users to click through.

Keywords And Headers *(H1, H2, H3...)* – Detailed Checklist

Primary and Secondary Keywords: Incorporate primary and secondary keywords naturally within your heading tags.

Hierarchy: Maintain a clear and logical hierarchy of heading tags, using keywords appropriately in each.

Keywords And Body Content – Detailed Checklist

Natural Inclusion: Use keywords naturally within the content, avoiding forced or artificial insertion, no keyword stuffing!

First 100 Words: Try to include the primary keyword within the first sentence, or at least, the first 100 words of your content.

SEO for Recruitment

Keywords And Url – Detailed Checklist

URL Structure: Incorporate the primary keyword in the URL, maintaining a clean and straightforward structure.

URL Length: Keep the URL concise, ideally under 60 characters, to ensure it displays correctly in search results.

Additional Tips

- **Synonyms and Variations:** Use synonyms and variations of your primary keyword to avoid repetitiveness and to capture more search queries.
- **Context Matters:** Ensure that the keywords are contextually relevant to the content. Irrelevant keyword use can be detrimental to user experience and SEO.
- **Do some Keyword Research:** You must avoid keywords with low, or zero search volumes. However much you think you know your market, your customers, however certain you are that a keyword is right, test it. Make sure people are searching for it, and in the volumes you need! Working with keywords that no one is searching for is a very common and classic mistake, that can go undetected for years!

By following these steps and keeping these practices in mind, you'll be able to optimise your content with keywords effectively, enhancing both its search engine visibility and its appeal to readers.

Importance of Title Tags and Meta Descriptions

Your website's first *'handshake'* with users. Title tags and meta descriptions are the bold headlines of your website's story – they're among the first things users and search engines encounter when they find your webpage. Essentially, they serve as a concise introduction to what your page is all about.

These web page elements provide search engines with concise summaries of what your page is about. Using the right meta tags the right way is all about communicating to the search engines:

- What your page is about.
- How to read it.
- Who should see it.

Think of your title tags and meta descriptions as the introductory paragraph of a great article. They set the stage for what's to come, beckoning users to read more. A well-crafted title tag can entice users to click through to your website.

Equally a well-crafted Title Tag can make the difference between someone clicking on your site or scrolling past it. Similarly, Meta Descriptions act like the intriguing summary on the back cover of a book, offering a glimpse into the content of your page and compelling readers to dive into the full story.

Together, these elements work as your website's first impression in search results. They're your opportunity to stand out in the crowded digital landscape and draw in your target audience. Let's dive in and learn how to master these crucial tools, ensuring your website not only gets found but also gets clicked.

Rules:

- **Title Tags:** Use the the title tag to summarize the page's content in 50-60 characters. Ensure its unique for each page.
- **Meta Descriptions:** This should be a concise summary *(around 150-160 characters)* of the page's content. Therefore, each page will have a different Meta Description. It often appears in search results, so make it compelling.

Importance of Title Tags and Meta Descriptions Checklists

Title Tags – General Checklist

Primary Keyword Inclusion: Ensure that the primary keyword is included, preferably at the beginning of the title tag.

- **Example:** *For a page about "Job Interview Tips," your title tag might start with "Job Interview Tips".*

Relevancy: The title tag should accurately represent the content of the page.

- **Example:** *If your page is a guide, use a title like "Ultimate Guide to Job Interview Tips" Instead of something vague like "Interview Advice".*

Length: Maintain a character length between 50-60 characters to ensure it displays correctly in search results.

- **Example:** *Essential Job Interview Tips for Success | RecruitmentHub*

Uniqueness: Every page should have a unique title tag to avoid duplicate content issues.

- **Example:** *For different job search categories, use "CV Writing Tips for Getting Interviews | RecruitmentHub", "Essential Job Searching Strategies | RecruitmentHub".*

Branding: Consider including your brand name in the title tag, ideally at the end.

- **Example:** *"Learn Effective Job Search Techniques | RecruitmentHub".*

Special Characters: Use special characters like "|", "-" sparingly to separate words or phrases clearly.

- **Example:** *"Job Search Guide: Tips, Tools, Strategies | RecruitmentHub".*

Special Characters: Use special characters like "|", "-" sparingly to separate words or phrases clearly.

- **Example:** *"Searching for Employment - Your Help Guide | RecruitmentHub".*

Testing: Regularly test different title tag configurations to find the most effective option.

- **Example:** *Try variations like "Master Job Interviews: Expert Tips | RecruitmentHub" and analyse user engagement.*

Meta Description – Genererald Checklist

Primary and Secondary Keyword Inclusion: Seamlessly integrate both primary and secondary keywords naturally in the meta description.

- *Example:* For a page about "Job Interview Tips," include both "Job Interview" and related keywords like "Interview Preparation".

Relevancy: Ensure the meta description accurately summarises the content found on the page.

- *Example:* "Discover essential job interview tips to help you succeed and impress employers."

Length: Keep the meta description between 150-160 characters to make sure it displays correctly in search results.

- *Example:* "Discover our top job interview tips and strategies. Prepare effectively and increase your chances of landing your dream job today with our expert advice!"

Uniqueness: Write a unique meta description for each page to avoid duplication and accurately reflect different page content.

- *Example:* For a CV writing page, "Discover our top job interview tips and strategies. Learn how to craft the perfect CV to catch the attention of recruiters and secure that job interview."

Call-to-Action (CTA): Consider including a compelling call-to-action to encourage users to click through to your page, such as inviting users to learn more, apply now, or download a guide.

- *Example:* ""Secured that job interview? Great, and well done. Now, read our expert job interview tips and increase your chances of success. Start preparing today!"

Readability: The meta description should be readable and written in an active voice to make the meta description engaging and easy to read.

- *Example:* ""Enhance your interview skills with our comprehensive tips. Master interviewing, prepare effectively, practice confidently, and succeed in your next interview."

Special Offers or USPs: If applicable, highlight any special offers, unique services, or advantages of your recruitment services.

- *Example:* "Sign up for our newsletter and get exclusive job interview tips and career advice directly to your inbox. Subscribe today and empower your professional journey"

Testing: Experiment with different meta description configurations to identify the most effective setup.

- *Example:* Test variations emphasising different aspects, like quality, price, or exclusivity, and monitor click-through rates.

Some Keyword Usage Examples

Let's take a look at some examples that put keywords to work.

Example 1 – Permanent Recruitment

Keyword: *Permanent recruitment services*

Title: *"Permanent Recruitment Services: Find Your Ideal Candidates"*

Meta Description: *"Use our expert permanent recruitment services designed to find the best candidates for you. Ensure hiring success with our tailored solutions. Contact us today!"*

Content: *Incorporate the keyword naturally in various sections, discussing the process of permanent recruitment, including job analysis, candidate sourcing, and the benefits of long-term employment. Highlight success stories and best practices for ensuring cultural fit and retention.*

Example 2 – Freelance Recruitment

Keyword: *Freelance recruitment services*

Title: *"Freelance Recruitment Services: Hire Top Freelancers Quickly"*

Meta Description: *"Explore our freelance recruitment service, find and hire the best freelancers for your projects. Speed up your hiring process and get the talent you need today!"*

Content: *Incorporate the keyword naturally in various sections, covering the flexibility and scalability of freelance recruitment, tips for managing freelance contracts, and case studies of successful freelance hires. Discuss the benefits of using freelance talent for project-based work and how to integrate freelancers into existing teams.*

Example 3 – Temp Recruitment

Keyword: *Temp recruitment services*

Title: *"Temp Recruitment: Flexible Staffing Solutions for Your Business"*

Meta Description: *"Use our temp recruitment services to fill short-term roles with qualified candidates. Our flexible staffing solutions keep your business agile and* responsive."

Content: Content: Incorporate the keyword naturally in various sections, explaining the advantages of temp recruitment for handling seasonal peaks and special projects. Provide tips for onboarding temp staff and maintaining productivity. Include examples of how businesses have successfully used temp workers to meet their staffing needs.

Example 4 – Executive Recruitment

Keyword: Executive recruitment services

Title: "Executive Recruitment Services: Secure Top Leadership Talent"

Meta Description: "Our executive recruitment services, find and hire top-level executives for your company. Ensure leadership success withs our specialised search and selection."

Content: Incorporate the keyword naturally in various sections, detailing the executive search process, from defining leadership needs to conducting thorough candidate evaluations. Highlight the importance of confidentiality and strategic alignment in executive recruitment. Share case studies of successful executive placements and their impact on company growth.

Example 5 – IT Recruitment

Keyword: IT recruitment services

Title: "IT Recruitment Services: Find The Right Expert Tech Talent"

Meta Description: "Discover our IT recruitment services to hire skilled professionals. Ensure your projects are delivered by top tech talent with our IT recruitment solutions."

Content: Incorporate the keyword naturally in various sections, discussing the challenges of IT recruitment, including skills shortages and rapid technology changes. Provide tips for assessing technical competencies and cultural fit. Highlight success stories of IT projects completed by recruited professionals and their contributions to business objectives.

Example 6 – Healthcare Recruitment

Keyword: *Healthcare recruitment services*

Title: *"Healthcare Recruitment: Hire Qualified Medical Professionals"*

Meta Description: *"Utilise our healthcare recruitment services to hire qualified medical professionals. Ensure your facility is staffed with top talent for optimal patient care."*

Content: *Incorporate the keyword naturally in various sections, covering the importance of credential verification and compliance in healthcare recruitment. Discuss strategies for attracting and retaining top medical talent. Include examples of successful placements in various healthcare settings and their impact on patient care quality.*

Example 7 – Finance Recruitment

Keyword: *Finance recruitment services*

Title: *"Finance Recruitment Services: Secure Top Finance Talent"*

Meta Description: *"Explore our finance recruitment services to hire top professionals. Ensure your operations are managed by experts with our tailored recruitment solutions."*

Content: *Incorporate the keyword naturally in various sections, detailing the specific skills and qualifications needed for finance roles. Provide insights into the recruitment process, including candidate screening and assessment methods. Share case studies of successful finance placements and their contributions to organisational financial health.*

Example 8 – Engineering Recruitment

Keyword: *Engineering recruitment services*

Title: *"Engineering Recruitment Services: Hire Skilled Engineers"*

Meta Description: *"Use our engineering recruitment services to hire skilled engineers. Ensure technical excellence for your projects with our specialized recruitment solutions."*

Content: *Incorporate the keyword naturally in various sections, explaining the challenges of engineering recruitment, including niche skills and project demands. Provide tips for evaluating engineering competencies and ensuring project fit. Highlight success stories of engineering projects completed by recruited professionals.*

Internal and Outbound Linking

Welcome to the interconnected world of internal and outbound linking, a pivotal aspect of SEO and user navigation. It's not just about linking for the sake of it but creating a network that enriches user experience and boosts your SEO efforts.

Internal Linking: Your Site's Pathways

Imagine your website as a sprawling library. Now, how do you make it easy for visitors *(and search engines)* to explore this library? That's where internal linking comes in. Internal links are like your personal librarians, guiding visitors from one book *(page)* to another, based on what they're interested in. These links create pathways that help users navigate your site effortlessly, keeping them engaged and exploring. But there's a bonus – search engines love this too! Internal linking helps search bots understand the structure of your site, the relationship between pages, and which pages are most important.

So, it's not just about linking for the sake of linking. You've got to be strategic about it. Linking to relevant, authoritative pages can boost the SEO value of both pages. It's like boosting each other's credibility in the eyes of search engines.

Outbound Linking: Extending the Conversation

Then, we step into the realm of outbound linking. Think of these as references you give to your website visitors, directing them to other authoritative and reliable sources. Outbound links show search engines that you're well-connected and provide value by offering additional, relevant information. But remember, it's about quality, not quantity. Linking to credible, high-quality sites not only enhances your website's credibility but also enriches the user experience.

Anchor Text: The Art of Link Labelling

And let's not forget the anchor text – those few words you click on to jump to another page. Choosing the right anchor text is crucial. It should be relevant, descriptive, and if possible, include a keyword that aligns with the linked page. This makes it easier for both users and search engines to understand what the linked page is about.

In this section, we're going to dive deep into how you can strategically use internal and outbound links to weave a network that benefits your website in terms of SEO and provides a roadmap for your visitors. From best practices in link placement to crafting the perfect anchor text, we'll cover it all. So, let's start linking wisely and make your website a well-navigated hub of information!

Rules:

- Link internally to relevant pages on your site to keep users engaged. When considering whether to link to a page, think how a visitor *(human or search engine)* would fall if they followed that link? They need to feel they've been sent to a useful relevant page and its clear why they were taken there. So, don't just link for the sake of it

- Link out to reputable sources when citing information. Google has specified guidelines to qualify outbound links for SEO. This is to guard against link schemes designed to game the algorithm.

- Use descriptive anchor text for links, avoiding generic terms like *"click here"*. Integrate links naturally within the content, using anchor text that clearly indicates what the linked content is about.

- Maintain a balanced approach by not overloading the page with too many links, while ensuring there are enough to aid navigation and provide additional information.

Internal and Outbound Linking Checklists

Internal Links – General Checklist

Relevant Linking: Link to pages within your site that offer additional value and are contextually related to the content.

- *Example:* In a blog post about 'Job Interview Tips', link to a related internal article like 'Top 10 CV Writing Tips'.

Natural Anchor Text: Use natural and descriptive anchor text that gives readers a clear idea of the linked content's topic.

- *Example:* Instead of "Click here," use "Read our comprehensive guide on preparing for interviews."

Logical Structure: Plan your site's internal linking to reflect a logical and hierarchical structure facilitating smooth navigation.

- *Example:* From your homepage, link to category pages such as 'Job Listings', and from those categories, link to individual job postings or articles on job search advice.

Link Depth: Avoid deep link structures; a user should reach any page in less than four clicks. Ensure users can access any page on your site within four clicks from the homepage.

- *Example:* Home > Services > Permanent Recruitment > Job Postings, each step being a click.

Avoid Broken Links: Regularly check and fix broken internal links *(404)* Use tools like Google Search Console to regularly scan for and fix any broken links to maintain a healthy website structure.

- *Example: If you find a broken link, either update it with a relevant, active page or remove the link if no suitable replacement exists.*

Link to High-Authority Pages: Distribute your site's authority effectively by linking to your most authoritative pages, like popular blog posts or key service pages.

- *Example: Link from newer blog posts or less visited pages to your most popular or cornerstone content, such as your 'Recruitment Services' page.*

Linking to Every Page: Ensure that every page on your site, particularly those you want to rank for, has at least two internal links pointing to it.

- *Example: On your 'About Us' page, include links to your 'Contact' page and a relevant blog post that tells more about your team or mission.*

External Links – General Checklist

Relevance: Ensure that all external links add value to your content and are directly related to the topic at hand.

- *Example: If you have a blog post about 'Job Market Trends in 2024,' link to a relevant research paper or news article on recent developments in the recruitment industry.*

High-Quality Sources: Ensure that you are only linking to high-quality, reputable, and authoritative websites to build trust and credibility with your audience.

- *Example: When citing statistics or facts, link to well-known industry publications, educational institutions, or government resources.*

Nofollow Attribute: Use the *"nofollow"* attribute judiciously for links where you do not want to pass link equity, such as untrusted content, affiliate, or paid links.

- *Example: For a product review with affiliate links, add rel="nofollow" to the anchor tag in the HTML.*

Open in New Tab: Configure external links to open in a new browser tab, keeping visitors on your site while allowing them to explore additional information.

- *Example:* In your blog's HTML code, add target="_blank" to the anchor tags of your external links, such as links to industry reports or external job boards.

Avoid Broken Links: Regularly check and fix broken outbound links to provide a seamless user experience.

- *Example:* If you find a broken outbound link, update it with a current, relevant source or remove the link if no alternative is available.

Anchor Text – General Checklist

Relevance and Descriptiveness: Ensure the anchor text is relevant to the content of the linked page. Use descriptive words that give users a clear idea of what they will find by clicking the link.

- *Example:* Instead of "Click here," use "Explore our permanent recruitment services."

Natural Integration in Content: Write anchor text as part of a sentence rather than forcing it in awkwardly. Make sure the anchor text naturally fits within the context of your content.

- *Example:* "For an in-depth analysis of this topic, read our comprehensive guide on effective interview techniques."

Variety and Diversity: Avoid using the same anchor text for different links. Use variations and synonyms to keep the anchor text diverse and natural.

- *Example:* If linking to a page about 'CV Writing Tips,' alternate anchor texts could be 'resume writing advice' or 'how to craft a perfect CV'.

Keyword Inclusion: Assess whether it's appropriate to include a keyword in the anchor text. Include relevant keywords in anchor text, but only when it aligns naturally with the content and linked page.

- *Example:* "Learn more about our IT recruitment services."

Avoid Generic Phrases: Look out for overuse of generic phrases like "click here" or "read more". Replace generic phrases with specific and informative descriptions.

- *Example:* Change "Click here for more info" to "Discover our latest job market trends report."

SEO for Recruitment

Length of Anchor Text: Ensure the anchor text is neither too short nor excessively long. Aim for concise yet descriptive anchor text, ideally between two to five words.

- *Example:* "Browse our current job openings."

No Over-Optimisation: Be cautious of over-optimising anchor text with too many keywords. Balance SEO needs with natural language to avoid seeming manipulative to search engines.

- *Example:* Avoid "best recruitment strategies for hiring improvement" in favor of "top recruitment strategies."

Image Optimisation

Painting a Thousand Words with Optimised Images. We all love crisp, beautiful images, but did you know they can also affect your site's load time and SEO? That's where image optimisation comes into play, and it's not just about making pictures look pretty.

In the digital landscape, images not only enhance the visual appeal of your webpage but, when optimised correctly, can play a pivotal role in improving your site's SEO.

Image optimisation is about reducing file sizes without compromising on quality, ensuring quick load times and a better user experience. Decreasing page load times, which is crucial for retaining users and improving SEO rankings. You can also improve the user experience and make your site more accessible to people with visual impairments using descriptive file names and alt attributes.

Rules:

- Always use descriptive file names *(e.g., "candidate-interview.jpg" rather than "image1.jpg")*.
- Use the *"alt text"* attribute to describe images; this helps search engines understand the image content and is vital for accessibility.
- Compress images to reduce file size without compromising quality. Tools like TinyPNG or Compressor.io can help.
- Use the appropriate image format *(e.g., PNG for more detailed images and JPEG for photographs)*.

Image Optimisation Checklists

Image Optimisation – General Checklist

Appropriate File Format: Choose the right format for each image type, to maintain a balance between quality and file size: JPEG for photos, PNG for graphics with transparency, WebP for a good balance, and AVIF for the latest compression technology.

- **Example:** Convert a portfolio photo from PNG to JPEG to reduce file size while maintaining quality.

Image Dimensions: Adjust the image dimensions to suit your website layout and avoid unnecessary large file sizes.

SEO for Recruitment

- **Example:** *If your blog content area is 800px wide, resize your images to this width.*

File Size: Compress images to reduce file size without compromising the quality significantly to improve page loading time.

- **Example:** *Use online tools like TinyPNG to compress an image while keeping it visually pleasing.*

Alt Text: Provide descriptive alt text for every image to improve accessibility and help search engines understand the content of the images.

- **Example:** *Instead of 'image1.jpg', use alt text like 'recruiter interviewing a candidate'.*

File Names: Use descriptive file names that reflect the image content, incorporating relevant keywords where possible.

- **Example:** *Rename 'DSC1002.jpg' to 'job-fair-recruitment.jpg'.*

Caption: If necessary, add captions to your images to provide more context and enhance user experience.

- **Example:** *Under a photo of a job fair, include a caption with details about the event and its significance.*

Responsive Images: Implement responsive image techniques to serve different image sizes for different devices and screen resolutions.

- **Example:** *Implement different image sizes for mobile, tablet, and desktop views.*

Lazy Loading: Enable lazy loading to defer the loading of off-screen images and improve page loading speed.

- **Example:** *Use the loading="lazy" attribute in your image tags.*

Load Time: Regularly check the load time of your pages and ensure that images are not slowing down your site.

- **Example:** *Identify images that significantly slow down your site and optimise them.*

Image Quality: Ensure that compression and resizing have not significantly diminished image quality.

- **Example:** *Compare the original and compressed images side by side to ensure the quality is still up to par.*

Broken Images: Regularly scan for and fix broken images to maintain a seamless user experience.

- **Example:** *Set up a monthly check with tools like Screaming Frog to ensure all images load correctly.*

Main Content

We know Google prioritises high quality content but what does that mean?

Step right into the heart of your website: the main content. The main content refers to the significant part of your webpage that delivers the value promised to your users through the title and meta description. This is your digital stage – where words, images, and media come together to not just tell a story, but to captivate and engage. But here's the twist: it's not only about dazzling your audience; it's about charming those search engines too.

Optimising the main content serves to fulfil a user's search intent: To address the needs and queries of your users proficiently. And boost SEO, to improve your webpage's standing in search engine results through quality content that search engines deem valuable.

User Intent: The North Star

Imagine having a conversation. You want to be sure you're not just talking at someone, but speaking to them, right? That's what aligning with user intent is all about. It's about crafting content that resonates, that answers the call of your audience's most pressing questions. Dive into the minds of your users – what are they searching for? What solutions do they need? That's your content's cue.

Structure and Formatting: The Backbone of Clarity

Now, let's get your content dressed for success. How you structure and format your writing can make a world of difference. Think of SEO like the reading glasses for search engines – your content needs to be clear and easy to digest. With well-placed headers, bullet points, and snappy paragraphs, you're not just organising your thoughts; you're paving a smooth path for search engines to follow and rank your content.

Multimedia: The Spice of the Digital World

Here's where the fun begins. Adding multimedia is like adding spice to a dish – it enhances and enlivens the experience. A picture here, a video there, maybe an interactive element to get hands-on – they all work together to transform your content from monochrome to HD. And the best part? Search engines love a good mix of media – it tells them your content is rich and engaging, which is just what they want to serve up in search results.

So, let's gear up to give your main content the attention it deserves. We'll be diving into the how's and why's of creating content that not only ticks all the SEO boxes but also gives your audience a reason to stay, explore, and interact. Ready to weave some content magic?

Before we get started, some good news, much of what you have learned already, will apply to your main content. For example, everything you know about keyword research applies to your main content. As this course has a strong focus on the practical, *'do this'* approach, for completeness we have cut no corners, so we knowingly repeat some rules, advice, and examples below, for example – Keyword Research.

Rules:

- Align with User Search Needs. The main content should directly address the needs or questions that brought users to your page.

- Make the Content *'Skimmable'*. Structure your content with headers, sub headers, bullet points and short paragraphs to break down information making it easier for readers to scan the page and find the information they need quickly.

- Use relevant Keywords. Strategically use keywords throughout the main content where they fit naturally. Include them in headers, near the beginning of the page, and sprinkled throughout the text to signal the page's topic to search engines.

- Ensure Mobile-Friendliness. With the prevalence of mobile browsing, your main content must read well on smaller screens. This means adapting the layout, image sizes, and interaction elements for mobile users.

There follows a series of checklists, for each aspect of your content that needs Optimising for search engines.

Content Checklists

Main Content Optimisation – General Checklist

Keyword Research: Identify primary and secondary keywords that are relevant to your topic. Integrate these keywords naturally into your content.

- *Example: For a post on "effective interview techniques," you might target keywords like "job interview tips" or "how to ace an interview."*
- *Refer to previous lessons on Keywords or for full understanding, our Keywords Simplified course.*

Content Structure: Organise your content with logical headings *(H1 for title, H2 for main points, etc.)*. Use bullet points and numbered lists for clarity where appropriate.

- *Example: Use H2 for "Preparing for an Interview" and H3 for specific tips like "Researching the Company."*
- *Refer to previous lessons on Headings and Tags.*

Readability: Write in short, clear sentences and paragraphs. Use everyday language to explain complex concepts. Write for you audience, not your peers – keep it simple, avoid jargon!

- *Example: Instead of large blocks of text, organise content with headers lists and bullet points.*

Incorporate Multimedia: Include relevant images, videos, and infographics to break up text and add visual interest.

- *Example: Well, chosen, appropriate, pictures (video's, infographics, etc) are worth a thousand words, do ensure all multimedia elements have been optimised for size and have SEO-friendly file names and alt text.*
- *Refer to previous lessons on Image Optimisation.*

Internal Linking: Link to other relevant pages or posts on your site to guide readers to more information. Use descriptive anchor text for all internal links.

- *Example: In your main content, you could turn the term "interview preparation" into a hyperlink linking to a page with an article on "top interview tips."*
- *Refer to previous lessons on Internal Linking.*

Call-to-Action: Include a clear call-to-action (CTA) that guides readers on what to do next. CTAs can be to subscribe, learn more, buy now, contact us, etc.

- *Example: "Ready to ace your next job interview? Download our free interview* checklist now!"

Meta Description: Write a concise meta description that includes the primary keyword and compels clicks. Keep it under 160 characters.

- *Example:* "Learn effective job interview techniques to impress employers and secure your dream job. Get expert tips and strategies here."
- *Refer to previous lessons on Meta Descriptions.*

Mobile Optimisation: Ensure your content is easily readable on mobile devices. Test loading times and display on various screen sizes.

- *Example: Ensure the website template or CMS (Content Management System) you are using is mobile-responsive. This means the content will automatically adjust to fit various screen sizes. If this is not the case, check with your web developers that your site and content is mobile optimised.*
- *Refer to upcoming lessons on Mobile Optimisation.*

Content Freshness: Regularly update content to keep it current and relevant. Refresh facts, figures, links, and statistics as needed.

- *Example: Update your "Top Interview Tips for 2024" post annually to include new and relevant advice.*

Content Length: Ensure your content is comprehensive enough to cover the topic effectively. Longer content tends to perform better in search engines but avoid fluff

- *Example: Write a thorough guide that answers all possible questions about starting a vegan diet, rather than a short, surface-level post.*

Quality Over Quantity: Focus on the value and quality of the information provided, not just on hitting a word count. Answer the reader's query fully and succinctly.

- *Example: Cut redundant explanations and get straight to the actionable advice or information the reader needs.*

Proofreading and Editing: Check for grammatical errors, spelling mistakes, and awkward phrasing. Use tools like Grammarly, or get a second pair of eyes to review your content.

- *Example: After writing your draft, take a break and come back to it with fresh eyes for proofreading, or ask a colleague to do so.*

Content Quality

High-quality content attracts and retains readers, leading to increased trust, longer page visits, and higher likelihood of social sharing and backlinks.

Rules:

- **Understand Your Audience.** Know who you're writing for and what they care about. Tailor your content to address their interests, challenges, and questions.
- **Deliver Value.** Ensure that the content is well-researched, informative, and free of grammatical errors, to provide accurate and comprehensive information.
- **Avoid** *"thin content"* which offers little to no value to the reader.
- **Organise the content logically** using headers and sub headers to facilitate easy reading.
- **Ensure content is original** and avoid duplicate content issues.

Content Quality Checklist

Content Quality – General Checklist

Audience Alignment: Ensure the content addresses the interests, needs, and pain points of the target audience. Tailor the tone, style, and complexity to the demographic you're serving.

- **Example:** If your audience is job seekers, create detailed content on resume writing, interview preparation, and job search strategies.

Value Proposition: Clearly define the unique value your content offers. Each piece should educate, inform, entertain, or solve a specific problem.

- **Example:** If there are many articles about job interview tips, your content could offer unique insights from industry experts or real-world success stories.

Comprehensiveness: Cover the topic in enough depth to fully satisfy the user's search intent. Include all necessary subtopics, questions, or related information users may expect.

SEO for Recruitment

- **Example**: A guide on job hunting should cover everything from crafting the perfect resume to negotiating job offers and onboarding.

Originality and Uniqueness: Create content that offers unique insights, not just a reiteration of what's already available. Use original research, case studies, personal anecdotes, or expert opinions to add value.

- **Example**: Use case studies from successful job placements or testimonials from clients who have benefited from your recruitment services.

Keyword Optimisation: Integrate primary and secondary keywords naturally within the content. Avoid overstuffing; focus on a natural, reader-friendly integration.

- **Example**: For an article on "executive recruitment," use variations like "hiring executives," "executive search services," etc.
- **Refer to previous lessons on Keywords, or Keywords Simplified course.**

Content Structure and Formatting: Organise content with clear headers and logical progression. Use bullet points, numbered lists, and bold text to highlight key information.

- **Example**: Break down a long article into sections with subheadings like "Benefits of Executive Recruitment" and "Steps to Hire Top Executives."
- **Refer to previous lessons on Content Structure, or Content Simplified course.**

Visual Appeal: Incorporate relevant images, videos, or infographics to complement the text. Ensure visual elements are high-quality and have proper titles and alt text.

- **Example**: Include infographics summarising key points of the hiring process or videos of expert interview tips.
- **Refer to previous lessons on Image Optimisation.**

Actionable Insights: Provide clear, actionable steps or key takeaways. Include checklists, tips, or how-to sections that empower readers to act.

- **Example**: After explaining the interview preparation process, provide a downloadable interview checklist.

Proofreading and Grammar: Ensure the content is free from spelling and grammatical errors. Use tools like Grammarly or Hemingway Editor for an additional layer of proofreading.

- **Example**: Before publishing, run the content through Grammarly and ask a colleague to review for clarity.

Mobile Optimisation: Verify that the content is easily readable on mobile devices. Test how the content displays on different screens and browsers.

- **Example:** *Use Google's Mobile-Friendly Test to see if your content is optimised for mobile users.*
- *Refer to upcoming lessons on Mobile Optimisation.*

Internal and External Links: Include relevant internal links to guide readers to additional content on your site. Cite authoritative external sources to add credibility and further information.

- **Example:** *Link to your "Resume Writing Guide" in a post about job application tips.*
- *Refer to previous lessons on Internal Links.*

Accuracy: Verify the accuracy of all statements and data, and cite trustworthy sources where necessary.

- **Example:** *Cross-check key facts and data against credible sources, and then update the content to reflect verified information. For example, if the article claims that "Networking can increase your job search success rate," reference and cite relevant studies or expert opinions to substantiate this claim.*
- *Refer to previous lessons on Internal Links.*

Content Freshness

Keeping Content Alive and Kicking. In the dynamic digital landscape, information constantly evolves. Maintaining the freshness of your main content ensures that your webpages stay relevant, updated, and in tune with the latest developments, meeting your audience's expectations for current and credible information. And accommodates the changing information needs of your users. Fresh, accurate content builds user trust, encouraging them to return to your website for reliable information.

Regularly updated content can be viewed as more relevant than stale content, and signals to search engines that your website is current, relevant, and valuable. Search engines like Google use "freshness" as a signal in their algorithms, positively influencing search engine rankings, and favour websites that are consistently updated with fresh content. This doesn't just mean adding new pages, but also revisiting and updating existing ones. Whether it's the latest industry news, recent developments, or just refining and expanding on what you've already published, keeping your content fresh helps maintain and improve your search rankings

Rules:

- Update blogs and articles periodically, especially when there are changes in the field.
- Consider a "Last Updated" date on pages to show recency.
- Maintain the relevance of the content by aligning it with current trends and user preferences.
- Regularly check and update outdated, or inaccurate links or information.
- Content Freshness Checklist

Content Freshness – General Checklist

Regular Content Audits: Schedule periodic audits *(monthly, quarterly)* to review and assess the freshness of your content. Identify pages that need updates, removal, or consolidation.

- **Example:** Monthly, check for pages with high bounce rates or low traffic, and list them for updates, such as outdated job market reports or recruitment tips.

SEO for Recruitment

Update Statistical Information: Regularly update any statistics or data in your content to reflect the most current information. Cross-check with the latest research or data sources.

- *Example:* If an article from 2020 cites employment statistics, update it with the latest year's data.

Refresh Outdated Content: Revise any content that references outdated information, trends, or news. Update examples, case studies, and references to be current and relevant.

- *Example:* Update a blog post about job search strategies to include the latest platforms and user behaviours.

Check and Update Internal and External Links: Ensure all internal and external links in your content are still relevant and working. Replace broken or outdated links with more current and relevant ones.

- *Example:* Use tools like Broken Link Checker to find and fix dead links, such as links to outdated job boards or industry reports.

Review SEO Keywords: Reevaluate the keywords used in older content. Update keywords to align with current search trends and user queries.

- *Example:* Replace old keywords with new ones identified by keyword research tools, aligning with current SEO best practices.

Enhance Content with New Insights: Add new sections or information to existing content based on recent developments or deeper insights. Provide additional value to the reader with expanded analysis or perspectives.

- *Example:* For a piece on recruitment trends, include the latest advancements in remote hiring technologies.

Improve Visual Elements: Update or add new images, infographics, or videos to make the content more engaging. Ensure all multimedia elements are optimised and relevant.

- *Example:* Replace an outdated infographic with a more modern, interactive one.

Re-promote Updated Content: Share refreshed content on social media and other platforms. Consider sending updated pieces in newsletters or other marketing channels.

- *Example:* Post the refreshed content on your social media with a note like "Updated with the latest recruitment trends!"

Implement Evergreen Strategies: Create or update content to be evergreen, maintaining relevance over time. Ensure that evergreen content remains comprehensive and authoritative.

- *Example:* Write a guide on "How to Prepare for a Job Interview" that focuses on timeless strategies rather than current trends.

Monitor User Engagement and Feedback: Track user engagement metrics *(e.g., time on page, engagement rate)* to identify content needing updates. Incorporate user feedback and comments into content updates.

- *Example:* If users comment asking for more information on a topic, update the content to include this, such as more detailed resume tips.

Establish a Content Calendar: Develop a content calendar that schedules regular updates for existing content. Plan new content that can complement and refresh older posts.

- *Example:* Set reminders to review key pages every quarter, such as your "Top Job Search Tips" page.

Document Content Changes: Keep a record of updates made to content for tracking purposes. Note major revisions with update dates on the webpage to inform readers.

- *Example:* At the end of an updated article, add a note like "Updated on [date] with the latest statistics on [topic]."

Technical SEO Best Practice

Technical SEO Best Practice Learning Objectives & Timings

Technical SEO Best Practices Introduction

Insights into technical SEO best practices, essential for enhancing your site's loading speed, security, and compatibility with mobile and other platforms, directly impacting your search engine rankings and overall user experience.

Timing: 10 minutes

Learning Objectives:

- **Understand the purpose of technical SEO** in supporting site performance and search engine rankings.
- **Identify key technical SEO best practices**, including loading speed, security, and mobile compatibility.
- **Recognise how technical SEO influences user experience** and contributes to higher search visibility.

Website Speed

The crucial role of website speed in technical SEO, where faster loading times significantly enhance user experience and contribute to higher search engine rankings by meeting the efficiency expectations of users and search algorithms alike.

Timing: 30 minutes

Learning Objectives:

- **Understand the impact of website speed** on both user experience and SEO performance.
- **Identify techniques for improving loading times** to meet user and search engine expectations.
- **Recognise how efficient website speed contributes to higher rankings** and sustained user engagement.

Mobile Optimisation

The importance of mobile optimisation in technical SEO, ensuring your site functions seamlessly on mobile devices, catering to the vast number of mobile users and positively influencing your website's search engine rankings.

Timing: 30 minutes

Learning Objectives:

- **Understand the role of mobile optimisation** in enhancing user experience for mobile device users.

- **Identify key techniques for ensuring seamless functionality** of websites on mobile devices.

- **Recognise how mobile optimisation contributes to higher search engine rankings** and accommodates the growing mobile user base.

Secure Website

The necessity of maintaining a secure and accessible website in the realm of technical SEO, emphasising how implementing HTTPS and ensuring easy site navigation not only protects your users but also boosts your standing in search engine results.

Timing: 30 minutes

Learning Objectives:

- **Understand the importance of website security** in protecting users and supporting SEO goals.

- **Recognise the role of HTTPS** in establishing a secure connection and improving search engine ranking.

- **Identify best practices for maintaining a secure and accessible site** that enhances user trust and meets SEO standards.

Accessible Website

Why accessibility matters. Understand and implement the principles of web accessibility through the lens of Technical SEO.

SEO for Recruitment

Timing: 30 minutes

Learning Objectives:

- **Understand the importance of web accessibility** in providing an inclusive experience for all users.
- **Identify key accessibility practices** that support SEO and improve user engagement.
- **Learn how to implement accessibility principles** to enhance both usability and search engine visibility.

Schema Markup

Explore the world of schema markup, a powerful yet often overlooked form of technical SEO that communicates the context of your content to search engines, enhancing the way your page displays in SERPs and improving click-through rates.

Timing: 30 minutes

Learning Objectives:

- **Understand the purpose of schema markup** in providing context to search engines about webpage content.
- **Identify the benefits of schema markup** for enhancing how pages are displayed in search engine results.
- **Recognise how schema markup can improve click-through rates** *(CTR)* by making search listings more informative and engaging.

URL Structure

Understand the impact of a well-crafted URL structure as a facet of technical SEO, highlighting how clear and concise URLs improve user experience, make site navigation intuitive, and assist search engines in understanding and ranking your content.

Timing: 30 minutes

Learning Objectives:

- **Recognise the importance of a clear and concise URL structure** in supporting both user experience and SEO.

SEO for Recruitment

- **Understand how effective URL structure aids search engines** in interpreting and ranking website content.
- **Identify best practices for creating intuitive, SEO-friendly URLs** that improve navigation and visibility.

Indexation

The concept of indexation in technical SEO, explaining how proper practices ensure search engines correctly process and store your website's pages in their index, making them available for displaying in relevant search results.

Timing: 30 minutes

Learning Objectives:

- **Understand the role of indexation** in making website pages accessible to search engines.
- **Recognise best practices for ensuring correct page indexation**, supporting visibility in search results.
- **Identify techniques to manage which pages are indexed** to optimise search engine performance and relevance.

Total Time to Complete Technical SEO Best Practices

Total Section Timing: 220 minutes
(excluding practical integration with your website)

Technical SEO Best Practices: Introduction

Welcome to the pivotal world of Technical SEO, where the behind-the-scenes work can make a monumental difference in your website's performance and search engine rankings. This section of our course is dedicated to unravelling the technical aspects of SEO, making them accessible and actionable for you.

Think of Technical SEO as the foundation of a house – it needs to be strong and well-built to support everything that sits on top of it. Here, we're not just talking about keywords and content; but rather focuses on enhancing the infrastructure of the website. We are delving into the core elements that make your website appealing to search engines, helping search engines crawl, interpret, and index your website pages more efficiently.

Why? Because a well-optimised technical foundation facilitates better search engine rankings and is pivotal in providing users with a seamless browsing experience.

The Pillars of Technical Optimisation

- We'll start by boosting your **Website Speed**, ensuring your site loads swiftly to keep both users and search engines happy. Slow load times are a no-go in today's fast-paced digital world.

- Next, we'll ensure your site operates flawlessly on mobile devices with **Mobile-Friendly Operation** techniques. With increasing internet browsing happening on mobile, this is no longer optional.

- Security and accessibility are paramount. We'll cover how to make your website **Secure and Accessible**, safeguarding user data and making sure everyone can access your content.

- Ever heard of **Schema Markup**? This is like a secret language that speaks directly to search engines, enhancing the way your site is represented in search results.

- We'll also refine your **URL Structure** for clarity and efficiency, making it easier for search engines to understand the layout and content of your site.

- The trio of **Indexation** – Optimised Robots.txt, comprehensive **XML Sitemap**s, and strategic use of Canonical Tags – ensures that search engines can effectively crawl and index your site.

SEO for Recruitment

- And we won't forget about handling the inevitable – **404 pages and 301 Redirects** – turning potential errors into opportunities for a seamless user experience.

This section is designed to equip you with the skills and knowledge to fine-tune these technical elements, enhancing your website's SEO performance from the ground up. Ready to dive in and get technical? Let's enhance your website's mechanics for an optimal SEO strategy!

Website Speed

A Speedier Website for a Better First Impression. Think of the last time you waited for a slow-loading website. Frustrating, wasn't it? In the fast-paced digital world, speed is king, and this is precisely where we begin our journey into Technical SEO. Welcome to Website Speed Optimisation – a crucial aspect that can significantly impact your site's user experience and SEO performance

Website speed isn't just a technical detail; it's a crucial component that can dictate the first impression your website leaves on a visitor. A fast-loading website offers a superior user experience, leading to higher engagement levels and conversion rates.

However, it is not all about the user experience, site speed is a significant factor in Google's search ranking algorithms, impacting your site's visibility in search results.

Why Speed Matters

Picture your website as a race car in the vast internet speedway. If it's not optimised for speed, it's like being stuck in the slow lane while your competitors zoom ahead. A fast-loading website isn't just about keeping your visitors happy; it's also about impressing search engines. Google loves speedy sites, often rewarding them with better rankings.

The Tools and Tricks

But how do you boost your website's speed? It's not as daunting as it sounds. We'll explore some straightforward yet powerful techniques. First, tools like Google PageSpeed Insights are your best friends. They provide valuable insights and actionable recommendations tailored to your website.

Optimising for Speed

Then, we dive into practical steps like compressing images – think of it as shedding unnecessary weight off your race car. We'll also talk about leveraging browser caching, which is like giving your users a turbo boost on subsequent visits, and minimising JavaScript and CSS files – akin to fine-tuning your engine for optimal performance.

So, are you ready to turbocharge your website? Let's dive into the nitty-gritty of Website Speed Optimisation and get your site up to speed – literally and figuratively!

Rules:

- **Minimise Code:** Streamline your site's code by removing unnecessary characters and whitespace.
- **Optimise Images:** Use compressed images and implement lazy loading to speed up page load times.
- **Leverage Browser Caching:** Store static files in the user's browser to reduce server lag.

Website Speed Checklist

Website Speed – General Checklist

Utilising Google PageSpeed Insights

What to Do:

Use Google PageSpeed Insights to analyse your website's performance.

How to Do It:

Enter your website's URL into the tool and run the analysis. The tool will provide a performance score and list specific areas for improvement.

Example:

You might find recommendations like "Eliminate render-blocking resources" or "Serve images in next-gen formats."

Utilising Google Analytics

What to Do:

Use Google Analytics to check page load times

How to Do It:

Check Google Analytics > Behaviour > Site Speed > Page Timings

SEO for Recruitment

Example:

- *What is the avg. page load time of the website? Is it alarming? More than 6s?*
- *What are the pages with a worse / slower load time compared to the site average?*
- *Which pages have high pageviews but a slower load time compared to the site average?*
- *Run this report to speed up the most important pages on your site first (top 10 pages).*
- *What are the suggestions in the 'Opportunities' section with the highest time savings?*
- *Group the opportunities by LCP, TBT, and CLS to see suggestions tackling the core web vitals.*
- *What are the pages with a worse / slower load time compared to the site average?*

AND... keep going and apply the following checks...

Compressing Images

What to Do:

Reduce the file size of images on your website without compromising quality.

How to Do It:

Use image compression tools such as TinyPNG or ImageOptim. You can also use Photoshop's "Save for Web" feature.

Example:

An image that is originally 2MB can often be compressed to below 500KB, significantly improving load times.

Website Speed – Specialist Checklist

The following are for the more technically minded. They aren't simple everyday tasks that the majority of SEO technicians are able to carry out, they are more geared to developers – none the less, they are important and if flagged in any scans or reports about your website, they could make a big difference to your overall optimisation.

These technical issues are beyond the scope of this course.

Leveraging Browser Caching

What to Do:

Set up your website so that it stores its static elements in users' browsers, reducing load times for repeat visitors.

How to Do It:

Modify your site's .htaccess file to set expiry times for certain types of files. This can often be done through plugins on platforms like WordPress.

Example:

Set images, CSS, and JavaScript files to cache for a month. When users return to your site, these files load from their cache rather than being downloaded again.

Minimising JavaScript and CSS Files

What to Do:

Reduce the size and number of JavaScript and CSS files on your site.

How to Do It:

Use tools to minify and combine your JS and CSS files. This means removing unnecessary characters and whitespace and combining multiple files into one.

Example:

Instead of having five separate CSS files, combine them into a single, minified file.

Implementing Lazy Loading

What to Do:

Set up your images and videos to load only as they're about to enter the viewport.

How to Do It:

Use a lazy loading script or feature. Many website development platforms and content management systems offer this as a built-in feature or as an add-on.

Example:

As a user scrolls down your page, images load just in time for the user to view them, instead of loading all images at initial page load.

Optimising Server Response Time

What to Do:

Improve your server's response time.

How to Do It:

Choose a quality hosting provider, consider a Content Delivery Network *(CDN)* for a global audience, and optimise your server *(like database optimisation)*.

Example:

If using a WordPress site, optimise your database by removing old post revisions and unused data.

Mobile Performance Optimisation

What to Do:

Ensure your site is optimised for mobile devices.

How to Do It:

Implement responsive design, compress images for mobile, and minimise the use of heavy scripts that may slow down mobile performance.

Example:

Test your site's performance on mobile devices using Google's Mobile-Friendly Test and make necessary adjustments based on the feedback.

Mobile Optimisation

Embrace the Mobile-first world. As more and more people browse the internet via smartphones, having a mobile-optimised website isn't just an added advantage—it's a necessity. A mobile-friendly site ensures you cater to the broadest audience possible, including the vast number of mobile users.

In this part of our journey through Technical SEO, we're focusing on making your website not just accessible, but a pleasure to use on mobile devices.

Why Mobile Matters

Imagine your audience is on the go, coffee in one hand and phone in the other. We want to ensure they can enjoy your website with the same ease as they would on a desktop. With the majority of internet browsing now happening on mobile devices, having a mobile-friendly site is no longer optional; it's imperative.

Plus, mobile optimisation is important for SEO rankings. Since September 2020 Google has been operating a *'Mobile-First Indexing'*, meaning Google predominantly uses the mobile version of the content for indexing and ranking, making mobile optimisation pivotal for SEO.

Responsive Web Design

The key here is responsive web design. This is like a one-size-fits-all outfit for your website; it looks great no matter what device it's viewed on. Responsive design automatically adjusts your site's layout, images, and content to fit various screen sizes perfectly.

Testing and Tweaking

And how do we know if we're getting it right? Enter Google's Mobile-Friendly Test. This nifty tool gives us a clear picture of how mobile-friendly our site is and where we can improve. It's like a mobile-readiness report card for your website.

So, are you ready to make your website a welcoming place for mobile users? Let's delve into the nuances of crafting a responsive design and ensure your site scores high on mobile usability. It's time to optimise your digital presence for thumbs and fingers scrolling on the go!

Rules:

- Responsive Design: Implement a responsive design that adapts to various screen sizes.
- Accessible Elements: Design elements such as buttons and links should be easily clickable on a mobile interface.

Mobile Optimisation Checklist

Mobile Optimisation – General Checklist

Adopting Responsive Web Design:

What to Do:

Ensure that your website adapts to different screen sizes and resolutions, providing an optimal viewing experience on all devices, from desktops to smartphones.

How to Do It:

Utilize responsive design frameworks like Bootstrap or Foundation, or, if you're using a content management system *(CMS)* like WordPress, choose a responsive theme. Ensure that your website's layout, images, and navigation menus adjust automatically to the user's device.

Example:

On a mobile device, your website's menu should switch to a hamburger menu (three horizontal lines), and content should reflow to fit the smaller screen without horizontal scrolling.

Using Google's Mobile-Friendly Test

What to Do:

Test your website's mobile usability to identify any issues affecting mobile viewers.

How to Do It:

Go to Google's Mobile-Friendly Test tool, enter your website's URL, and analyse the results. The tool will provide feedback on any mobile usability problems, such as text that's too small, elements too close together, or the use of incompatible software.

Example:

After entering your website's URL into the tool, you might find that the text is too small to read on mobile devices. The tool will recommend increasing the font size for mobile users.

Optimising Images and Media:

What to Do:

Ensure that all images and multimedia content are optimised for fast loading and proper display on mobile devices.

How to Do It:

Compress images and use responsive image solutions *(like the HTML srcset attribute)* so that the appropriate image size is served depending on the user's screen. For videos, use responsive embedding so that they scale correctly on mobile devices.

Example:

Instead of having one large image file, create multiple versions of the image in different sizes. The browser will then load the most suitable size for the user's screen.

Simplifying Navigation

What to Do:

Make sure the navigation on your mobile site is straightforward and easy to use.

How to Do It:

Opt for a simple, streamlined navigation menu on mobile. Large, easy-to-tap buttons are a must. Consider implementing a sticky menu that moves with scrolling for easy access.

Example:

Convert your desktop site's multi-level menu into a single-level dropdown menu on mobile. Check you have adapted content formats suitable for mobile viewing, including shorter paragraphs and bullet points.

Touch-Friendly Design

What to Do:

Design your website so that all interactive elements are easy to tap on a touch screen.

How to Do It:

Increase the size of buttons and clickable areas. Ensure there's enough space around links to prevent mis clicks.

Example:

Make sure buttons like 'Submit', 'Read More', or social media icons are large enough to be easily tapped on a small screen.

Testing on Real Devices

What to Do:

Beyond using online tools, test your website on actual mobile devices for firsthand experience.

How to Do It:

Access your website on various smartphones and tablets to check for usability, readability, and navigation ease. Get feedback from actual users if possible.

Example:

Borrow different mobile devices from friends or colleagues and navigate your website, paying attention to loading times, image display, and the ease of using menus and buttons.

Core Web Vitals – Largest Contentful Paint *(LCP)*

What It Is:

LCP measures the loading performance of a website, specifically how long it takes for the largest content element *(like an image or text block)* to load. Ensure your page's main content loads within 2.5 seconds to offer a good user experience.

How to Optimise:

- Compress and optimise images without losing quality.

- Use lazy loading for images and non-critical resources.
- Minimise server response times by using a reliable web host and considering the use of a Content Delivery Network *(CDN)*.

Example:

If your homepage features a large hero image, compress the image file, and implement lazy loading so that it doesn't slow down the initial page load.

Core Web Vitals – First Input Delay *(FID)*

What It Is:

FID measures interactivity, specifically the time from when a user first interacts with your site to the time when the browser responds to that interaction. Keep your pages' first input delay under 100 milliseconds to maintain interactivity.

How to Optimise:

- Minimise or defer JavaScript until it's needed.
- Remove any non-critical third-party scripts.
- Use a web worker to run some JavaScript tasks in the background.

Example:

If your website uses a JavaScript-based slider, ensure the JavaScript loads after the main content, so it doesn't delay the site's initial interactivity.

Core Web Vitals – Cumulative Layout Shift *(CLS)*

What It Is:

CLS measures visual stability, focusing on how much content shifts on the page unexpectedly. Aim for a CLS score below 0.1 to avoid disruptive content shifts.

How to Optimise:

- Ensure images and embeds have dimensions specified in the HTML.
- Avoid inserting new content above existing content unless in response to a user action.
- Minimise animations or dynamic content that causes layout shifts.

SEO for Recruitment

Example:

If you have ads or images that dynamically load and cause content to shift, specify their dimensions in advance to prevent layout shifts.

Secure Website

Building Trust through Safety and Security. In today's digital landscape, securing your website isn't just about protecting your business assets; it is also about building trust with your audience.

The primary objectives of ensuring website security and accessibility are:

- **Protecting Data:** Safeguarding sensitive data from unauthorised access.

The focus on security has benefits for SEO, search engines favour websites that are secure, enhancing their ranking in search results. And benefits for building user trust and confidence, users are more likely to trust and engage with a website that is secure and can be accessed easily.

This is where HTTPS comes into play, turning your website into a secure haven for visitors. Think of HTTPS as the sturdy lock on your front door, ensuring that everyone who enters feels safe and protected.

Why HTTPS Matters

In an age where data breaches and online threats loom large, securing your website with HTTPS isn't just a nice-to-have; it's a must. It encrypts the data transferred between your visitors and your website, safeguarding sensitive information from prying eyes. Not just that, search engines like Google give a nod of approval to secure sites, often ranking them higher.

SSL Certificates: Your Website's Shield

The key to this security is an SSL *(Secure Sockets Layer)* certificate. It's like a digital passport that provides authentication for your website and enables an encrypted connection. No more worrying about data interception or tampering.

Getting Set Up

Thankfully, setting up HTTPS is straightforward. Most hosting providers offer SSL certificates, and many even include them for free with their hosting packages. It's about reaching out to your provider and following a few simple steps to get that certificate up and running on your site.

So, ready to make the leap to a more secure, trustworthy website? Let's walk through the process of securing your site with HTTPS, a critical step in fortifying your online presence and building trust with your audience. It's time to turn the key and unlock a safer, more secure user experience.

Rules:

- **SSL Certificate:** Install an SSL certificate to transition your site to HTTPS, securing data transfer.
- **XML Sitemap:** Create and submit an XML sitemap to help search engines understand the structure of your website.
- **Regular Updates:** Frequently update your website's software to mitigate vulnerability to security breaches.

Secure Website Checklist

Secure Website – General Checklist

Updating Your Content Management System *(CMS)*

What to Do:

Regularly update your CMS to the latest version.

How to Do It:

- Check for updates in your CMS dashboard. Most systems like WordPress, Joomla, or Drupal notify you of available updates.
- Always back up your website before applying updates.

Example:

If you use WordPress, updates can typically be done with a few clicks from the Dashboard > Updates section.

Updating Plugins and Themes

What to Do:

Ensure all your website plugins and themes are updated to their latest versions.

How to Do It:

- Regularly check your CMS for updates to plugins and themes. Prioritise updates that mention security fixes.

Example:

For a WordPress site, go to Plugins > Installed Plugins and Themes > Themes, and update any that have a new version available.

Updating Server Software and Scripts

What to Do:

Keep your server software and any scripts you use up to date.

How to Do It:

- This often involves working with your hosting provider. For scripts, use official sources to download updates.
- For server software, your host might handle updates, or you may need to manually update via your server control panel.

Example:

If you're using a PHP script on your website, ensure you're running the latest PHP version supported by your hosting service.

Obtaining an SSL Certificate

What to Do:

Acquire an SSL certificate for your website. This digital certificate will activate the padlock and the HTTPS protocol, ensuring secure connections from a web server to a browser.

How to Do It:

- Contact your hosting provider. Many offers free SSL certificates as part of their hosting packages.
- For more advanced needs, consider purchasing an SSL certificate from reputable authorities like Let's Encrypt, Comodo, or Symantec.
- Follow your provider's instructions to implement the certificate on your site.

SEO for Recruitment

Example:

If you're using a hosting service like Bluehost or SiteGround, you can often enable SSL directly from your hosting dashboard with just a few clicks.

Installing the SSL Certificate

What to Do:

Install the SSL certificate on your web server.

How to Do It:

- This process varies depending on your hosting environment. Generally, it involves accessing your web server or hosting control panel, navigating to the security section, and uploading your certificate files.
- In some cases, you might need to update your web server configuration.

Example:

On a cPanel hosting environment, you would click on 'SSL/TLS' in the security section, then go to 'Manage SSL Sites' to install your certificate.

Ensuring Complete HTTPS Implementation

What to Do:

Ensure all website elements are served over HTTPS to avoid mixed content issues *(where some elements are loaded over an insecure HTTP connection).*

How to Do It:

- Update internal links, images, scripts, and CSS files to use HTTPS URLs. Utilise tools like *'Whynopadlock'* to check for and identify any mixed content issues.

Example:

Change all instances of 'http://www.yoursite.com' to 'https://www.yoursite.com' in your website's source code.

Redirecting HTTP to HTTPS

What to Do:

Set up a 301 redirect from HTTP to HTTPS so that users and search engines are directed to the secure version of your site.

How to Do It:

- Modify your website's .htaccess file or use your hosting control panel to set up the redirect.

Example:

Add a rule in your .htaccess file that redirects any HTTP requests to HTTPS.

Updating Your Site's Settings

What to Do:

Update your website's settings to reflect the change to HTTPS.

How to Do It:

- If you're using a CMS like WordPress, update the site URL and home URL to use HTTPS in the General Settings.

Example:

Change the WordPress Address and Site Address from 'http://www.yoursite.com' to 'https://www.yoursite.com'.

Notifying Search Engines:

What to Do:

Update your sitemap and notify search engines of your switch to HTTPS.

How to Do It:

- Resubmit your updated sitemap through tools like Google Search Console.

Example:

Submit a new sitemap via Google Search Console to ensure Google indexes your HTTPS pages.

Accessible Website

Here we look at a vital and often overlooked aspect of Technical SEO – making your website universally accessible. In this section, we will embark on a journey to understand and implement the principles of web accessibility through the lens of Technical SEO. It's about building a digital space that everyone, regardless of their abilities, can navigate, understand, and enjoy.

Why Accessibility Matters in SEO

Imagine entering a building with no ramp – how would someone in a wheelchair feel? The same principle applies to websites. Web accessibility ensures that all users, including those with disabilities, have equal access to information and functionality. This is not just about social responsibility; it's about reaching a wider audience and enhancing your website's usability, which search engines like Google increasingly prioritise.

There's one more, primary objective, of ensuring website accessibility:

- **Compliance:** Adhering to legal and regulatory requirements that advocate for digital inclusivity.

The Technical Roadmap

The realm of Technical SEO provides us with tools and techniques to improve accessibility. From optimising site navigation to ensuring content is easily readable and understandable, we'll cover the technical adjustments that make a significant impact. These enhancements not only cater to users with specific needs but also refine the overall user experience, contributing positively to your site's SEO performance.

Practical and Impactful Changes

We'll dive into practical steps such as using alt text for images, ensuring keyboard-friendly navigation, and implementing ARIA *(Accessible Rich Internet Applications)* roles. These changes go a long way in making your website more inclusive.

Testing and Compliance

Lastly, we'll explore how to test your website for accessibility issues and ensure compliance with standards like WCAG (Web Content Accessibility Guidelines). Tools and techniques to continually monitor and improve your site's accessibility will be a key focus.

Get ready to make your website not just a destination but a welcoming, inclusive community for all your visitors. Enhancing your website's accessibility is a journey that benefits everyone and boosts your SEO efforts. Let's begin this journey towards creating a more accessible and SEO-friendly website.

Rules:

- **Implement and Maintain Responsive Design:** A responsive design adapts to different screen sizes and orientations, providing an optimal viewing experience on a variety of devices, including smartphones and tablets. This is crucial for users with varying degrees of visual and motor skills.

- **Optimise for Universal Design and Navigation:** XML Sitemap: Ensure your website is navigable and functional for all users, including those using screen readers, keyboard navigation, and other assistive technologies. This includes logical structure, clear headings, keyboard-friendly navigation, and meaningful link text.

- **Ensure Content Clarity and Readability:** Use clear, straightforward language and ensure all multimedia content *(images, videos)* is complemented with descriptive text, like alt text for images. Structure your content with proper headings and provide transcripts or captions for audio and video content.

- **Accessibility Checks:** Perform periodic checks using accessibility tools to ensure compliance with WCAG guidelines.

Accessible Website Checklist

Accessible Website – General Checklist

Understanding WCAG Levels

What to Do:

- Ensure the website meets the legal requirements and guidelines such as Web Content Accessibility Guidelines *(WCAG)*
- Familiarise yourself with the different levels of WCAG compliance: A *(basic)*, AA *(standard)*, and AAA *(highest)*.

How to Do It:

- Review the guidelines on the W3C website and determine which level of compliance is most appropriate for your website.

Example:

- *Most businesses aim for AA compliance as it balances reasonable accommodation with technical feasibility.*

Use of Alt Text for Images

What to Do:

- Provide descriptive alt text for all images on your website.

How to Do It:

- Add a concise description in the alt attribute of the image tags. This description should convey the purpose or content of the image.

Example:

- *For an image of a laptop on a desk, the alt text could be "Laptop with notepad and pen on a wooden desk."*

Ensuring Keyboard Navigation

What to Do:

- Make sure your website can be navigated using a keyboard alone.

How to Do It:

- Regularly test your site using keyboard navigation. Ensure all interactive elements are accessible and that the focus order is logical.

Example:

- *Users should be able to tab through menu items and select them using the Enter key.*

Readable and Understandable Content

What to Do:

- Ensure that the language on your website is easy to read and understand.

How to Do It:

- Use clear and simple language. Break up text into short paragraphs and use bullet points for easier reading.

Example:

- *Avoid jargon and complex sentences, especially in important informational content like product descriptions.*

Proper Use of Headings

What to Do:

- Structure your content using proper heading tags *(H1, H2, H3, etc.).*

How to Do It:

- Use H1 for the main title, H2 for main sections, and H3s for subsections. Ensure headings are descriptive and in a logical order. Ensure there is only one h1 tag for each page? And ensure the h2 – h6 tags are optimised with keywords *(long-tail keywords, related keywords).*

Example:

- *On a blog post, the H1 could be the post's title, each major section starts with an H2, and subtopics under each section are marked with H3s.*

Accessible Forms

What to Do:

- Make sure all forms on your site are accessible.

How to Do It:

- Label all form fields clearly, ensure error messages are descriptive, and that forms can be navigated using a keyboard.

Example:

- *For a sign-up form, each input field should have a corresponding label, like "Email Address."*

Use of ARIA *(Accessible Rich Internet Applications)* Roles

What to Do:

- Implement ARIA roles and attributes where appropriate to enhance accessibility, especially for dynamic content and advanced user interface controls.

How to Do It:

- Use ARIA roles to define the type of UI component and states for screen readers.

Example:

- *For a dropdown menu, use the ARIA role 'menu' and define 'menuitem' roles for each dropdown item.*

Contrast and Colour Considerations

What to Do:

- Ensure there is sufficient contrast between text and background colours.

How to Do It:

- Use tools like the WebAIM Contrast Checker to verify that your text is easily readable against its background.

Example:

- *Avoid light grey text on a white background; instead, use darker colours for your text.*

Accessible Multimedia

What to Do:

• Provide captions and transcripts for audio and video content.

How to Do It:

• Include closed captioning for videos and transcripts for podcasts and audio files.

Example:

• *For a tutorial video, offer a text transcript or captions that describe both the spoken content and relevant non-verbal sounds.*

Testing and Validation

What to Do:

• Regularly test your website's accessibility.

How to Do It:

• Use accessibility testing tools like WAVE or AXE and consider manual testing by users with disabilities.

Example:

• *Run your website through the WAVE tool to identify potential accessibility issues and rectify them.*

Schema Markup

Imagine walking into a library where every book is meticulously categorised and easy to find. That's the kind of clarity and organisation Schema Markup brings to your website in the vast digital library of the internet. Welcome to the world of Structured Data Implementation – a pivotal part of Technical SEO that helps search engines understand your content better and display it attractively in search results.

Decoding Schema Markup

Schema Markup is like a behind-the-scenes guide for search engines, providing explicit clues about the meaning of a page's content. It's a form of structured data that tells search engines not just what your data says, but what it means. Whether it's an article, a product listing, an event, or a recipe, Schema Markup helps search engines display your content in a way that stands out.

The Rich Snippets Advantage

Ever noticed those eye-catching results in Google with star ratings, images, or additional information? Those are rich snippets, powered by Schema Markup. By implementing structured data, you can enhance the appearance of your website in search results, potentially increasing click-through rates and driving more traffic to your site.

Getting Started with Implementation

It is worth understanding the basics of schema markup and its importance in SEO, identify the types of schema markup that are relevant to your website content *(e.g., article, product, event, local business)*.

Define the scope of schema markup implementation — deciding which pages and content types will have schema markup. And identify and familiarise yourself with the necessary tools *(such as Google's Structured Data Markup Helper)* for schema markup implementation.

Don't worry, you don't need to be a coding wizard to get started with Schema Markup. We'll guide you through how to identify the right Schema types for your content and how to implement them using tools and plugins, making your pages more informative and appealing to search engines.

So, are you ready to help search engines better understand and showcase your content? Let's dive into the nuts and bolts of Schema Markup and Structured Data Implementation and give your website the spotlight it deserves in search results.

Rules:

- Identify the right schema type for your content. Schema.org provides a comprehensive list of schemas to choose from based on the kind of content your webpage has.
- Correctly implement the schema markup on your website, ensuring that all necessary properties are included. Use Google's Structured Data Markup Helper for assistance.
- Avoid marking up content that is not visible to users, as this can be seen as deceptive and result in penalties.
- Regularly update the schema markup to ensure that it accurately reflects the current content on your webpage.
- Test your markup with Google's Structured Data Testing Tool.

Schema Markup Checklist

Understanding Schema Markup Implementation – General Checklist

Understanding Schema Markup

What to Do:

- Familiarise yourself with Schema.org, the central repository for structured data vocabularies used to markup content for search engines.

How to Do It:

- Visit Schema.org and explore the different types of Schema markup available, such as Article, Product, Event, and Recipe.

Example:

- *If you run a cooking blog, you'll want to understand the Recipe schema, which allows you to markup elements like ingredients, cooking time, and nutritional information.*

Select The Right Schema Markup – General Checklist

Selecting the Right Schema

What to Do:

- Choose the appropriate Schema type that matches the content of your page.

How to Do It:

- Identify the main theme of your page and match it with a corresponding Schema type.

Example:

- *For a product page on an e-commerce website, use the Product schema to markup information like price, availability, and customer reviews.*

Schema Generation Tools – General Checklist

Using Tools for Schema Generation

What to Do:

- Utilise online tools to generate Schema markup.

How to Do It:

- Tools like Google's Structured Data Markup Helper can guide you in creating and implementing the markup.
- Ensure the correct syntax *(JSON-LD or Microdata)* is used while creating the schema markup.
- Include all required properties for the chosen schema type to avoid errors.
- Utilise optional properties to provide additional information and enhance your

content's structured data.

- Where possible, set up dynamic fields to automatically update schema properties such as price or availability.

Example:

- Use the Structured Data Markup Helper to select the type of data (like a product or event), paste the URL of your page, and use the tool to tag different elements. The tool then generates the appropriate JSON-LD markup that you can add to your page.

Schema Markup Implementation – General Checklist

Implementing Schema Markup

What to Do:

- Add the chosen Schema markup to your webpage's HTML.

How to Do It:

- You can manually add JSON-LD *(recommended by Google)*, Microdata, or RDFa formats to your HTML code. Alternatively, use CMS plugins or tools to simplify the process.

Example:

- *Add JSON-LD structured data to a product page, including elements like the product name, description, price, and review ratings.*

Schema Markup Testing – General Checklist

Testing Your Implementation

What to Do:

- After implementing Schema markup, test it to ensure its correctly recognised by search engines.

How to Do It:

- Enter the URL of your marked-up page into the test tool (Google's Rich Results

Test tool or Google's Structured Data Testing Tool) to validate your structured data.
- Test the schema markup across different browsers to ensure consistency and correct rendering.
- Ensure the schema markup is correctly implemented and accessible on mobile devices.

Example:
- *Validate the schema markup and ensure it is error-free. Enter the URL of your marked-up page into the test tool. The tool will show whether the page is eligible for rich results and highlight any errors in your markup.*

Schema Markup Integration – General Checklist

CMS Integration
- Integrate schema markup into your CMS to streamline the implementation process for future content.

SEO Plugins
- Utilise SEO plugins that facilitate easy schema markup implementation, if applicable.

Schema Markup Maintenance – General Checklist

Search Console
- Regularly check Google Search Console for any schema markup errors or issues.

Updates
- Stay updated with the latest changes and updates to schema markup guidelines and implement necessary adjustments.

Feedback and Reviews

- Encourage and integrate user reviews and ratings through schema markup to enhance your content's credibility and appeal.

URL Structure

Imagine if you were given a map with clear and straightforward directions to your destination. That's exactly what a well-structured URL does for both your users and search engines. Welcome to the segment on URL Structure, where we dive into the art of creating clean, efficient, and SEO-friendly URLs for your website.

The Backbone of Your Website. In the world of SEO, where competition is fierce and attention spans are short, the structure of your URLs can be a decisive factor in determining the success or failure of your SEO strategy. URL structure plays a pivotal role in ensuring a smooth user experience and aiding search engines in deciphering the content and context of your webpage effectively.

URLs should be short, descriptive, and include the target keyword for the page. This helps both search engines and users understand a page's relevance. Use hyphens to separate words for readability and use a consistent URL structure across the site.

The Importance of URL Structure

In the grand scheme of Technical SEO, URL structure might seem like a small detail, but it packs a significant punch. A well-crafted URL not only tells your visitors and search engines what the page is about immediately but also improves user experience and site navigation. It's like giving everyone a mini guide to what to expect before they even land on the page.

Keeping It Clear and Descriptive

The key is to keep your URLs concise, descriptive, and peppered with relevant keywords. This is not just for the sake of SEO; it's about making your site more navigable and your content more accessible.

Reflecting Site Hierarchy

Structuring your URLs to mirror your site's hierarchy helps users understand where they are on your site and how to navigate to related content. It's like building a well-organised filing system where everything is logically placed and easy to find.

Avoiding the Pitfalls

We'll also tackle common mistakes to avoid, like overly lengthy URLs, confusing parameters, or cryptic strings that leave users guessing.

So, are you ready to roll up your sleeves and fine-tune your URLs? Let's break down the essentials of creating URLs that are not just search engine friendly but also make sense to your human visitors. It's time to shape up your URLs and pave the way for better navigation and SEO.

Rules:

- **Descriptive URLs:** Use descriptive URLs that clearly indicate the content of the page.
- **URL Length:** Keep URLs concise and avoid unnecessary long strings.

URL Structure Checklist

Url Structure – General Checklist

Consistency

- Ensure a consistent URL structure across your website for better user experience and SEO.

Simplicity

- Keep URLs simple, avoiding unnecessary complexity or length.

Keywords

- Include primary keywords in URLs to reinforce the topic of the page and improve SEO.

Hyphens

- Use hyphens (-) to separate words in URLs, making them easier to read for both users and search engines.

Avoid Special Characters

- Refrain from using special characters in URLs, which can cause issues with browsers and aren't SEO-friendly.

-

Link Checking

Regularly check for broken links and fix them promptly to maintain website health.

URL Testing

Test URLs to ensure they load correctly and efficiently, without any errors.

Creating Concise and Descriptive URLs

What to Do:

- Ensure each URL is easy to read and gives a clear idea of what the page is about.

How to Do It:

- Use straightforward language and include relevant keywords. Avoid long strings of numbers or characters.

Example:

- *Instead of website.com/page123, use website.com/resume-writing-tips.*

Reflecting Site Hierarchy in URLs

What to Do:

- Structure your URLs to mirror the navigational hierarchy of your website.

How to Do It:

- Organise your website content into clear categories and subcategories and reflect this structure in your URLs.

Example:

- *For a blog post under the category 'Career Advice' and the subcategory 'Job Interviews', use: website.com/career-advice/job-interviews/interview-tips.*

Keeping URLs Consistent

What to Do:

- Use a consistent, predictable URL structure across your website.

How to Do It:

- Develop a standard URL structure template for different types of content (like blog posts, job listings, etc.).

Example:

For blog posts, you might always use the format website.com/blog/post-title.

Redirecting Old URLs After Changes:

What to Do:

- If you update URLs, set up 301 redirects from the old URL to the new one.

How to Do It:

- Use .htaccess file *(for Apache servers)* or appropriate tools in your CMS to implement 301 redirects.

Example:

- *If you change website.com/aboutus to website.com/about-us, ensure the old URL redirects to the new one.*

Using Hyphens to Separate Words:

What to Do:

- Use hyphens, not underscores or spaces, to separate words in URLs.

How to Do It:

- In your CMS or when manually creating URLs, ensure words are separated by hyphens.

SEO for Recruitment

Example:

- *Use website.com/job-search-tips instead of website.com/job_search_tips.*

Url Structure: Pitfalls To Avoid – General Checklist
Overuse of Keywords

Pitfall:

- Stuffing URLs with too many keywords can appear spammy to both users and search engines.

How to Avoid:

- Use keywords judiciously. Include your primary keyword in a way that naturally describes the page's content.

Example:

- *Avoid website.com/job-job-search-job-interview-job-preparation, instead use website.com/job-preparation-tips.*

Complex and Confusing Structure

Pitfall:

- Creating URLs with too many levels or confusing paths can make it hard for users and search engines to understand the page hierarchy.

How to Avoid:

- Simplify the URL structure. Reflect your site's navigation hierarchy, but don't make URLs excessively long or complex.

Example:

- *Instead of website.com/services/recruitment/permanent/staffing/industry/specific, a simpler version could be website.com/permanent-staffing.*

Inconsistent URL Structures

Pitfall:

- Using different URL structures for similar pages can create confusion and hinder site coherence and SEO.

How to Avoid:

- Standardise a URL structure template for your website and stick to it.

Example:

- *If your blog posts use website.com/blog/post-title, ensure all posts follow this format.*

Using Session IDs in URLs

Pitfall:

- Session IDs in URLs can lead to duplicate content issues and cluttered URLs.

How to Avoid:

- Configure your website to store session information in cookies rather than in the URL.

Example:

- *Avoid URLs like website.com/page?sessionid=12345. Ensure session data is not included in the URL.*

Lengthy URLs with Unnecessary Parameters

Pitfall:

- Keep URLs short and free of unnecessary parameters or session IDs that can clutter the URL.

How to Do It:

- Limit the use of URL parameters unless they are essential for tracking or functionality. Configure your CMS or server settings to create cleaner URLs.

Example:

- *IConvert website.com/jobsearch?type=fulltime&location=nyc to website.com/fulltime-jobs-nyc.*

Dynamic URLs with Excessive Parameters**Pitfall:**

- URLs with a lot of parameters *(like ?id=123&sort=asc)* can be off-putting to users and difficult for search engines to crawl.

How to Avoid:

- Whenever possible, turn dynamic URLs into user-friendly static URLs. Use URL rewriting techniques.

Example:

- Convert *website.com/jobs?category=it&type=fulltime* to *website.com/it-fulltime-jobs*.

Neglecting Case Sensitivity

Pitfall:

- Inconsistent use of capitalisation in URLs can lead to duplicate content issues, as some servers treat different cases as separate URLs.
- Keep all characters in your URLs lowercase to avoid confusion, as URLs are case-sensitive.

How to Avoid:

- Always use lowercase letters in URLs.
- Configure your CMS settings to generate lowercase URLs, or manually ensure URLs are lowercase.

Example:

- Use *website.com/about-us*, not *website.com/About-Us*.

Ignoring URL Redirection After Changes

Pitfall:

- Failing to redirect old URLs after making changes can lead to broken links and negatively impact SEO.

How to Avoid:

- Implement 301 redirects from old to new URLs whenever changes are made.

Example:

- *If you update a URL, ensure the old URL redirects to the new one to preserve link equity and user access.*

Indexation

The process through which search engines like Google find, analyse, and store information from web pages in their vast databases, called *"indexes."* When a page is in the index, it is in the running to be displayed as a result to relevant queries. Proper indexation is a cornerstone of SEO because if a page isn't indexed, it won't appear in search engine results, no matter how well-optimised it is.

Gain a fundamental understanding of what indexation is and why it's vital for SEO. Then document the important URLs of your site which should be indexed.

Use of Robots.txt

Starting with Optimised Robots.txt, think of it as the gatekeeper that instructs search engine crawlers on which parts of your site to explore and which to bypass. It's a critical tool for guiding crawlers efficiently and preventing them from accessing irrelevant or sensitive areas of your site.

Rules:

- **Allow:** Ensure important pages are allowed for crawling.
- **Disallow:** Use this directive to prevent search engines from indexing non-essential pages, like admin pages.

Robots.txt Checklist

Robots.txt – General Checklist

Robots.txt

- Locate your site's robots.txt file *(typically in the root directory)*. If it doesn't exist, create a new text file named robots.txt.

Set Rules

- Specify which areas of your site should or shouldn't be crawled using *"Disallow"* and *"Allow"* directives.
- Check that important pages are allowed for crawling in the robots.txt file.
- Used *"Disallow"* directive to prevent indexing of non-essential pages *(like admin pages)*.

Robots.txt Example

User-agent: *
Disallow: /private/
Allow: /public/

XML Sitemaps

Next, XML Sitemaps act like a GPS for search engines, to assist search engines in understanding the structure of your website and indexing it more effectively, providing a structured layout of your website's pages.

This ensures that no important page is missed during the crawling process, especially vital for larger sites with numerous pages.

Rules:

- **Update Regularly:** Keep the sitemap updated with all the significant changes on your website.
- **Submit to Search Engines:** Submit your XML sitemap to search engine webmaster tools, like Google Search Console, for better indexation.
-

XML Sitemaps Checklist

Xml Sitemaps – General Checklist

Creation

- Create an XML sitemap, use a sitemap generator tool or CMS plugin. This sitemap should list URLs of all important pages on your site.

Sitemap Submission

- Submit your sitemap to search engine webmaster tools, such as Google Search Console and Bing Webmaster Tools.

Regular Updates

- Regularly update the XML sitemap when you make major changes to your website.

XML Sitemaps Example

- *If you have one, an XML sitemap can generally be accessed at website.com/sitemap.xml*

Canonical Tags

With Canonical Tags, we tackle the challenge of duplicate content. These tags help you tell search engines which version of a similar webpage is the 'official' one, preventing confusion and preserving your site's integrity in search results.

Rules:

- **Specify Preferred URL:** Use canonical tags to indicate the preferred version of a URL.
- **Self-Referencing Canonical Tags:** Implement self-referencing canonical tags to affirm the master version of a page.

Canonical Tags Checklist

Canonical Tags – General Checklist

Identify Duplicate Content

- Look for pages with identical or very similar content.

Preferred URL's

- Identified and specified preferred URL versions using canonical tags.
- In the head section of each duplicate page's HTML, add a canonical link element pointing to the preferred URL.

Self-referencing tags

- Implement self-referencing canonical tags to establish the master version of a page.

Consistent Use

- Always use Canonical Tags when creating duplicate content.

Canonical Tags Example

- <link rel="canonical" href="https://www.website.com/ptreferred-page" />

404 Page and 301 Redirects

Lastly, we delve into the world of 404 error management and 301 Redirects. Here, we transform potential dead ends (like deleted or moved pages) into smooth redirections, enhancing user experience and maintaining the flow of link equity throughout your site.

Rules:

- **301 Redirect:** Use this to permanently direct users from a deleted or moved page to a new or relevant page.
- **Custom 404 Page:** Create a custom 404 page to guide users back to working sections of your site if they land on a non-existent page.

404 Redirects Checklist

404 And 301 Redirects – General Checklist

Identify Moved or Deleted Content
- Find URLs that have been moved or removed

Implement redirects
- Consistently implement redirects for deleted or moved pages to new or relevant pages

404 redirects
- Create a custom 404 page to guide users back to active sections of your site if they land on a non-existent page

Page Experience

Page Experience Learning Objectives & Timings

Page Experience – Introduction

How this aspect of technical SEO plays a crucial role, focusing on a user's interaction with a page and how it is perceived, which can directly influence overall satisfaction and search engine rankings.

Timing: 10 minutes

Learning Objectives:

- Understand the significance of page experience in influencing user satisfaction and search engine rankings.
- Identify key elements that contribute to a positive page experience, such as loading speed, interactivity, and visual stability.
- Recognise how page experience impacts SEO, improving both user engagement and search visibility.

Core Web Vitals

Examine Core Web Vitals, key metrics in technical SEO and essential components of page experience that measure the quality of a user's engagement with a webpage, impacting your site's ranking and overall online performance.

Timing: 30 minutes

Learning Objectives:

- Understand the role of Core Web Vitals as critical metrics in evaluating page experience and SEO performance.
- Identify the main components of Core Web Vitals—such as loading speed, interactivity, and visual stability.
- Recognise how optimising Core Web Vitals can positively impact your site's search rankings and user engagement.

Mobile Friendliness

The importance of mobile-friendliness, a critical factor in technical SEO that ensures your website's optimal performance on mobile devices, reflecting directly on user satisfaction and search engine rankings in an increasingly mobile-centric world.

Timing: 30 minutes

Learning Objectives:

- Understand the importance of mobile-friendliness in enhancing user experience on mobile devices.
- Recognise how mobile optimisation influences search engine rankings in a mobile-first indexing environment.
- Identify best practices for ensuring mobile-friendly design and functionality, contributing to improved SEO and user satisfaction.

Safe Browsing and https

The significance of safe browsing and the implementation of HTTPS in technical SEO, safeguarding user data and establishing trust while positively influencing your website's search engine rankings by adhering to the 'secure-by-default' standard online.

Timing: 30 minutes

Learning Objectives:

- Understand the role of safe browsing and HTTPS in protecting user data and enhancing website security.
- Recognise how implementing HTTPS establishes trust with users and aligns with search engine security standards.
- Identify best practices for maintaining a secure website, contributing to improved SEO rankings and user confidence.

Total Time to Complete Page Experience

- **Total Section Timing:** 100 minutes *(excluding practical integration with your website)*

Page Experience – Introduction

What is Page Experience

In addition to quality content and good technical SEO, it's crucial to optimise the overall experience users have when visiting your web pages. Page Experience is a set of signals that Google uses to gauge the experience users have on a webpage. It involves a range of factors including how fast the page loads, its mobile-friendliness, safety of browsing and HTTPS security.

Optimising these factors leads to better user engagement and satisfaction. It also improves organic search rankings since metrics like page speed are top evaluation criteria for search engines like Google. Users expect fast, mobile-friendly, and secure websites.

In this section, we'll cover easy tips to:

- Improve your Core Web Vitals factors – page load time, interactivity and visual stability – through performance optimisations
- Ensure your website is fully responsive and mobile-ready
- Implement HTTPS encryption and SSL certificates

Why Does Page Experience Matter?

Ever visited a website that took forever to load or was hard to navigate on your phone? Frustrating, isn't it? That's precisely what we aim to avoid. Search engines like Google prioritise websites that provide a positive experience, as they want to direct users to pages that not only answer their queries but are also a pleasure to use. A great Page Experience means happier visitors, potentially leading to better engagement, higher rankings, and more conversions.

Core Web Vitals

The page experience signals that have been a Google ranking factor since June 2021.

Now, some SEO people get very hooked up on core web vitals and will tell you that it is the be all and end all that your web site pages score highly here or that's the end of any SEO efforts. We don't get so hooked up, and in our experience, high scores in Core Web Vitals don't often lead to additional rankings or targeted traffic.

Core Web Vitals do contain a lot of information about the performance of your website. It's almost all technical information about the way things load, the time it takes for them to load, the size of files and much more. So, there is something to be taken from them, just not everything. If you go down the path to complete everything Core Web Vitals says you should change, we can guarantee you'll wish you hadn't and you'll rarely, if ever, get to the end of the path.

Google retrieves Core Web Vitals field data from a public source called the Chrome User Experience Report (CRuX). This information originates from users who've chosen to share their browsing records and turned-on usage statistics reporting – that is, in our opinion, already a hit-and-miss data set that may, or may not, contain your target audience.

So, this raises a pertinent question: Are Core Web Vitals, as indicators of user experience, leaning towards Chrome users? Given that the benchmarks are determined by Chrome user data, how reflective is this of the experience on different browsers like Firefox and Safari? Could Core Web Vitals be inaccurately portraying the user experience for Firefox or Safari users, awarding good ratings in Chrome, while the actual experience on other browsers might be more, or less, satisfactory?

It's essential to recognise that, currently, CRuX is the sole public dataset of its kind. Should other browsers release similar datasets, a broader and more balanced assessment of genuine user experience would be achievable. For now, Google relies on the data at hand. It would be prudent for anyone to seek broader methods to evaluate UX, even other Google products such as Google Analytics to analyse metrics across various browsers.

SEO for Recruitment

Rules

- **LCP:** Optimise Largest Contentful Paint to be under 2.5 seconds, ensuring that the main content of your page loads quickly.
- **FID:** Maintain a First Input Delay under 100 milliseconds to guarantee smooth interactivity.
- **CLS:** Keep Cumulative Layout Shift below 0.1 for a stable visual page content layout.

Core Web Vitals Checklist

Core Web Vitals – General Checklist

Largest Contentful Paint *(LCP)*

What It Is:

- LCP measures the loading performance of a website, specifically how long it takes for the largest content element *(like an image or text block)* to load.
- Ensure your page's main content loads within 2.5 seconds to offer a good user experience.

How to Optimise:

- Compress and optimize images without losing quality.
- Use lazy loading for images and non-critical resources.
- Minimize server response times by using a reliable web host and considering the use of a Content Delivery Network *(CDN)*.

Example:

- *If your homepage features a large hero image, compress the image file and implement lazy loading so that it doesn't slow down the initial page load.*

First Input Delay *(FID)*

What It Is:

- FID measures interactivity, specifically the time from when a user first interacts with your site to the time when the browser responds to that interaction.
- Keep your pages' first input delay under 100 milliseconds to maintain interactivity.

How to Optimise:

- Minimize or defer JavaScript until it's needed.
- Remove any non-critical third-party scripts.
- Use a web worker to run some JavaScript tasks in the background.

Example:

- *If your website uses a JavaScript-based slider, ensure the JavaScript loads after the main content, so it doesn't delay the site's initial interactivity.*

Cumulative Layout Shift *(CLS)*

What It Is:

- CLS measures visual stability, focusing on how much content shifts on the page unexpectedly.
- Aim for a CLS score below 0.1 to avoid disruptive content shifts.

How to Optimise:

- Ensure images and embeds have dimensions specified in the HTML.
- Avoid inserting new content above existing content unless in response to a user action.
- Minimize animations or dynamic content that causes layout shifts.

Example:

- *If you have ads or images that dynamically load and cause content to shift, specify their dimensions in advance to prevent layout shifts.*

Mobile Friendliness

We have talked about Mobile-Friendliness throughout this course, and in a previous module, so, here's a recap, and approaching the subject from a slightly different angle may help with understanding how to implement Mobile-Friendliness.

In a world where smartphones are as essential as our wallets, having a mobile-friendly website is no longer a luxury, but a necessity. Think about how often you use your phone to browse the web. Your website needs to not just exist, but shine on these smaller screens.

Mobile friendliness is a critical component of on-page SEO as it directly impacts a website's usability and search engine rankings, especially with the prevalence of mobile browsing. Google's mobile-first indexing approach prioritises mobile-optimised sites, making mobile friendliness essential for achieving higher rankings. Additionally, a mobile-friendly website enhances user experience, significantly influencing factors like dwell time and bounce rate, which are important for SEO.

In this section, we'll guide you through the essentials of making your website responsive, meaning it automatically adjusts its layout, images, and content to fit different screen sizes. We'll also cover how to ensure your site is just as navigable and interactive on a touchscreen, along with strategies to keep it loading quickly – a critical factor for mobile users on the go.

Rules

- **Responsive Design:** Implement a responsive design that adapts to various screen sizes.
- **Accessible Elements:** Design elements such as buttons and links should be easily clickable on a mobile interface.

Mobile Friendliness Checklist

Mobile Friendliness – General Checklist

Responsive Design

What to Do:

- Create a website layout that adapts and reflows to fit the screen size of various devices, from desktops to smartphones.

How to Do It:

- Use a responsive web design framework like Bootstrap or Foundation or select a responsive theme if you're using a CMS like WordPress.
- Test your site's responsiveness using tools like Google's Mobile-Friendly Test.

Example:

- *On a responsive site, a three-column layout on a desktop might stack into a single column on a mobile device, ensuring content is readable and navigation is straightforward.*

Touchscreen Navigation

What to Do:

- Make sure all interactive elements of your website are easily operable on a touchscreen.

How to Do It:

- Increase the size of buttons and links for easy tapping.
- Ensure there is enough space between interactive elements to prevent accidental taps.

Example:

- *Convert small drop-down menus into larger, finger-friendly buttons or menu sliders on the mobile version of your site.*

Mobile Speed Optimization

What to Do:

- Enhance the loading speed of your website on mobile devices.

How to Do It:

- Compress images and use modern formats like WebP.
- Minimize the use of heavy scripts and bloated code.
- Implement techniques like lazy loading for images and videos.

Example:

- *A photography blog can reduce the file size of images displayed on mobile devices, ensuring faster loading times without compromising on visual quality.*

Testing and Refining

What to Do:

- Continuously test and refine your website's mobile experience.

How to Do It:

- Use real mobile devices in addition to emulators for testing.
- Gather feedback from mobile users and adjust based on their experiences.

Example:

- *Regularly check how new blog posts or product pages appear and function on different smartphones and tablets, adjusting layouts or interactive elements as needed.*

Using Google's Mobile-Friendly Test

What to Do:

- Test your website's mobile usability to identify any issues affecting mobile viewers.

How to Do It:

- Go to Google's Mobile-Friendly Test tool, enter your website's URL, and analyse the results. The tool will provide feedback on any mobile usability problems, such as text that's too small, elements too close together, or the use of incompatible software.

Example:

- *After entering your website's URL into the tool, you might find that the text is too small to read on mobile devices. The tool will recommend increasing the font size for mobile users.*

Touch-Friendly Design

What to Do:

Design your website so that all interactive elements are easy to tap on a touch screen.

How to Do It:

- Increase the size of buttons and clickable areas. Ensure there's enough space around links to prevent mis clicks.

Example:

- *Make sure buttons like 'Submit', 'Read More', or social media icons are large enough to be easily tapped on a small screen.*

Mobile SEO Considerations

What to Do:

- Implement SEO best practices specifically for mobile.

How to Do It:

- Ensure meta titles and descriptions are concise and effective for mobile SERPs.
- Consider the impact of mobile user behaviour on SEO, such as shorter queries and voice search.

Example:

- *Optimise your site's metadata for clarity and impact within the limited space of mobile search results, using concise and engaging language.*

Safe Browsing and https

We have talked about Safe Browsing and Website Security throughout this course, and in a previous module, so, here's a recap, and approaching the subject from a slightly different angle may help with understanding how to implement website security.

In an era where digital security is paramount, ensuring your website is a haven for visitors is more crucial than ever. Welcome to the essential section on Safe Browsing and HTTPS, where we delve into the art of securing your online presence and building trust with your audience.

The Importance of a Secure Website

Imagine your website as a trusted place where visitors can freely interact, exchange information, and make transactions without fear. This level of trust is the foundation of Safe Browsing – it's all about creating a secure environment free from malware, phishing, and other online threats. A safe website not only reassures your visitors but also reflects positively on your brand and search engine rankings.

HTTPS: The Seal of Security

In today's internet landscape, having an HTTPS-secured website is the standard, not an option. It encrypts the connection between your visitors and your website, protecting sensitive data from being intercepted. Moving from HTTP to HTTPS is like upgrading from a simple door lock to a high-security system, essential for maintaining privacy and integrity.

Why This Matters? SEO and User Trust Go Hand in Hand

Recognizing the interplay between user trust and search engine optimization is key. Search engines favour secure websites, seeing them as reliable sources of information. By implementing HTTPS, you're not just securing data; you're boosting your SEO efforts.

Practical Steps to Enhance Security

We'll walk you through practical measures to implement Safe Browsing protocols and shift your site to HTTPS. From choosing the right SSL certificate to understanding the nuances of web security, this section demystifies the process and provides you with actionable steps to secure your website.

Prepare to dive into the essentials of web security. By the end of this section, you'll be equipped to create a safer, more secure, and SEO-friendly website that instils confidence in every visitor.

Rules:

- **SSL Certificate:** Install an SSL certificate to transition your site to HTTPS, securing data transfer.
- **XML Sitemap:** Create and submit an XML sitemap to help search engines understand the structure of your website.
- **Regular Updates:** Frequently update your website's software to mitigate vulnerability to security breaches.

Safe Browsing and HTTPS Checklists

Safe Browsing – General Checklist

Monitor for Security Issues

What to Do:

- Actively check your website for any signs of security breaches, including malware, phishing attempts, and other threats.

How to Do It:

- Regularly use security scanning tools. Google Search Console is an excellent resource; its Security Issues report can alert you to any potential risks.
- Consider using additional security monitoring services that can provide real-time alerts.

Example:

- *Set up weekly security scans through tools like Sucuri or Wordfence for a WordPress site. Regularly review any alerts or issues flagged by these tools.*

Implement Security Measures

What to Do:

Protect your website with robust security measures to prevent attacks and breaches.

How to Do It:

Install and configure security plugins if you're using a CMS. For WordPress, plugins like Wordfence or iThemes Security are popular choices.

Utilize web application firewalls (WAF) to protect against common vulnerabilities like SQL injection and cross-site scripting (XSS).

Ensure all your website software, including your CMS, plugins, and themes, are up to date.

Example:

If you're running an online store on WordPress, use a combination of a security plugin and a WAF service like Cloudflare to add an extra layer of protection.

Educate Your Users

What to Do:

Inform your users about safe browsing practices and how to protect their data while using your website.

How to Do It:

Create a dedicated section or page on your website with tips on safe browsing and data protection.

Clearly display your privacy policy and terms of service, ensuring they are easily accessible and written in plain language.

Example:

On a blog, include a sidebar or footer link to a 'Safety Tips' page, and ensure your privacy policy is clearly linked in your site's footer.

Https – General Checklist

Acquire and Install an SSL/TLS Certificate

What to Do:

- Secure your website by installing an SSL *(Secure Sockets Layer)* or TLS *(Transport Layer Security)* certificate.

How to Do It:

- Contact your web hosting provider about acquiring an SSL certificate. Many offer free SSL certificates through Let's Encrypt, or you can purchase one.
- Once you have the certificate, install it on your server. This process varies depending on your hosting platform, but generally involves accessing your hosting control panel and following the steps to install the certificate.

Example:

- *For a small business website hosted on a platform like Bluehost, you can activate a free SSL certificate directly from the hosting dashboard.*

Redirect HTTP to HTTPS

What to Do:

- Ensure all traffic to your website uses the secure HTTPS protocol.

How to Do It:

- Set up 301 redirects in your .htaccess file *(for Apache servers)* or equivalent on other servers to redirect all HTTP traffic to HTTPS.
- Update all internal links, canonical tags, and your sitemap to use HTTPS URLs to avoid mixed content issues.

Example:

- *If your website has a page http://www.example.com/about, add a 301 redirect rule so it automatically redirects users to https://www.example.com/about.*

Updating Your Site's Settings

What to Do:

- Update your website's settings to reflect the change to HTTPS.

How to Do It:

- If you're using a CMS like WordPress, update the site URL and home URL to use HTTPS in the General Settings.

Example:

- *Change the WordPress Address and Site Address from 'http://www.yoursite.com' to 'https://www.yoursite.com'.*

Verify and Test Your HTTPS Setup

What to Do:

- Check that your SSL/TLS certificate is installed correctly and your site is functioning properly over HTTPS.

How to Do It:

- Use SSL validation tools like SSL Labs' SSL Test to ensure your certificate is correctly installed.
- Regularly test your website to confirm that HTTPS is working on all pages, and look out for any mixed content warnings.

Example:

- *After setting up HTTPS on your online store, run the SSL Test and browse through different pages of your site to ensure all resources (images, scripts, stylesheets) are loaded over HTTPS.*

Notifying Search Engines

What to Do:

- Update your sitemap and notify search engines of your switch to HTTPS.

How to Do It:

- Resubmit your updated sitemap through tools like Google Search Console.

Example:

- *Submit a new sitemap via Google Search Console to ensure Google indexes your HTTPS pages.*

Key Learning Points and Take-Aways

The culmination of your SEO journey! As you wrap up, it's important to consolidate the essential insights and strategies you've learned. This course should have equipped you with not only the technical skills but also the strategic mindset necessary to elevate your website's search engine visibility effectively. Let's recap some of the crucial learning points and takeaways that you can apply immediately to make a tangible impact.

Key Learning Points and Takeaways

- **Understanding Your Audience:** Know who your customers are. Tailoring your SEO strategies to meet the specific needs and behaviors of your target audience is crucial for success.

- **Holistic SEO Approach:** SEO is holistic, not just enhancing your website but serving as an integral part of your marketing and business development. Both on-page and off-page SEO are vital, each element complementing the other to create a comprehensive, effective strategy that enhances your site's visibility and ranking.

- **Beyond Aesthetics:** Building a website isn't just about aesthetics; technical SEO is crucial. Ensure your site is not only visually appealing but also technically optimised to meet search engine standards.

- **Consistency is Key:** Maintain consistency in your SEO efforts. Regular updates and consistent application of SEO best practices are necessary to sustain and improve your rankings.

- **Security Matters:** Implementing robust security measures, like HTTPS, protects your users and boosts your SEO rankings, as search engines favor secure websites.

- **Keyword Optimisation:** Effective use of keywords remains a cornerstone of SEO. Identify and utilise the right keywords to improve your visibility and attract the right traffic to your site.

- Structured SEO Framework: Understanding the structure of SEO—how different components like meta tags, headers, and URLs work together—helps in optimising each element efficiently.

- **Content and Visibility:** Great content alone isn't enough; it must be supported by strong SEO to be seen. Don't let your valuable content go unnoticed due to inadequate optimisation.

- **Avoid Being a Secret:** Work on your visibility. Don't be the 'best kept secret.' Utilise SEO to ensure the right people find you through search engines.

- **Patience and Persistence:** SEO requires patience. Results may not be immediate, and understanding that SEO is a long-term investment is key. Allow time for changes to take effect and continually monitor the impact of your strategies.

- **Constant Review:** Regularly review your SEO outcomes to understand how search engines view your site and who they are directing to it. Assess whether your traffic consists of potential customers or just casual visitors, and adjust your tactics accordingly.

- **Empowerment Through Education:** While you can handle 80% of SEO tasks yourself, the remaining 20% might require deeper technical knowledge or more advanced training. Keeping up with SEO developments is crucial, especially if you manage multiple websites.

As we conclude the SEO for Recruitment course, remember that SEO is a continuous learning process. The digital landscape is always evolving, and staying informed is key to maintaining and enhancing your site's performance. Use the knowledge you've gained here to grow your online presence. And remember, the journey to SEO mastery doesn't end here—there are always new techniques to learn and apply. Keep experimenting, keep learning, and keep optimising. Your effort to expand your visibility is crucial in turning your website into a powerful asset for your business.

SEO for Recruitment

How Much Have You Learned?

Congratulations on reaching the final test of the SEO for Recruitment course!

This test is designed to test the knowledge you've gained throughout the course and to challenge your understanding of key SEO principles. Here are a few details to keep in mind as you prepare to take this important step:

Test Format: The test consists of 26 questions, some of which require selecting multiple correct answers. These questions are designed to be more challenging, ensuring you have a deep understanding of the course material.

Time Limit: Give yourself 45 minutes to complete the test. This time limit is set to encourage focus and efficiency, so make sure you are prepared and distraction-free before you begin.

Passing Score: The recommended passing score for the test is 80%. We encourage you to aim for 100% to demonstrate full mastery of the material. Achieving a high score is not just about passing the test; it's about ensuring you are fully prepared to apply SEO best practices in real-world scenarios.

Review and Learn: If you do not achieve the score you hoped for, use the remainder of your course access to review the content and strengthen your understanding. This test is a learning tool, designed to highlight areas that may require more attention.

You are prepared, good luck! Let's take the test!

1. **Which of these are goals of on-page SEO?** *(mutiple answers)*

A) Acquiring backlinks from other websites

B) Optimising internal content and structure for search engines

C) Enhancing the website's crawlability and indexing

D) Creating visually appealing graphics for the website

E) Improving the website's usability for users

Your Answer:

2. **Which of the following are ways On-Page SEO contributes to content marketing efforts?** *(mutiple answers)*

    A) It focuses solely on optimising content for search engines, not users.

    B) It ensures content is structured and written in a way that provides value to the audience.

    C) It reduces the need for off-page SEO strategies.

    D) It aligns content with search intent, attracting relevant traffic.

    E) It increases the number of internal links per page.

Your Answer:

3. **Why is the synergy between on-page and technical SEO crucial for a comprehensive SEO strategy?**

    A) It enhances both the foundation and content visibility, leading to better overall performance.

    B) It primarily increases website design flexibility.

    C) It reduces the need for keyword optimisation.

    D) It focuses only on increasing backlinks.

Your Answer:

4. **Which of these is not an example of the synergy between on-page and**

SEO for Recruitment

technical SEO?

A) Page Load Speed and Image Size: Optimising image sizes *(on-page)* improves page load speed *(technical)*, enhancing overall site performance.

B) Mobile Responsiveness and Content Layout: Adapting content layout *(on-page)* for mobile devices *(technical)* improves user engagement.

C) Structured Data and Rich Snippets: Applying structured data markup *(technical)* to content *(on-page)* can lead to rich snippets in search results.

D) URL Structure and Keyword Optimisation: Crafting URLs with keywords *(technical)* complements on-page keyword optimisation, strengthening the keyword strategy.

E) Meta Descriptions and Internal Linking: Meta descriptions *(on-page)* provide enticing summaries, while internal linking *(on-page)* helps guide visitors across the site.

Your Answer:

---

5. **Which of the following statements about HTTPS are true?** *(mutiple answers)*

   A) HTTPS is an important ranking factor that can improve SEO.

   B) HTTPS directly affects website design.

   C) HTTPS only impacts websites that handle sensitive transactions.

   D) HTTPS provides a secure foundation, enhancing user trust.

Your Answer:

---

6. **What impact does duplicate content have on SEO?**

   A) It directly leads to severe penalties from search engines.

   B) It may dilute content visibility in search results.

   C) It enhances SEO by providing more entries in search results.

   D) It improves SEO rankings by covering more topics.

Your Answer:

SEO for Recruitment

7. **Which of the following statements about technical SEO audits are true?**

    A) Technical SEO audits identify and rectify SEO issues, maintaining optimal website performance.

    B) Technical SEO audits ensure websites comply with international laws.

    C) Technical SEO audits increase the number of keywords used on each page.

    D) Technical SEO audits enhance the visual design of the website.

    E) None of the above.

Your Answer:

8. **What is the primary benefit of aligning site architecture with internal linking strategies?**

    A) It increases the number of external backlinks automatically.

    B) It facilitates more effective crawling by search engines and improves user navigation.

    C) It makes all links lead to the homepage for consistency.

    D) It allows for more frequent content updates.

    E) It improves a website's loading speed.

Your Answer:

9. **Which of the following best describes the role of link building in Off-Page SEO?** *(mutiple answers)*

    A) It creates backlinks from other websites, signalling to search engines the content's value and authority.

    B) It exclusively increases organic traffic by driving visitors directly to the website.

    C) It primarily affects internal linking strategies within the website.

    D) It improves the website's authority and reputation in the digital ecosystem.

    E) It can boost search engine rankings through endorsements from reputable websites.

Your Answer:

SEO for Recruitment

10. **Which of these are examples of the synergy between social media and technical SEO?** *(mutiple answers)*

    A) Social media engagement boosts brand visibility, indirectly driving traffic to the website, which can enhance SEO performance.

    B) Social media sharing can lead to backlinks from other websites, contributing to the website's SEO.

    C) Social media interactions improve a website's ranking in search engine results directly.

    D) Social media engagement increases the likelihood of the content being noticed by influencers, potentially leading to valuable backlinks.

    E) Social media content can increase the likelihood of a site ranking well for specific keywords.

Your Answer:

11. **Which of these are part of the role of meta descriptions in On-Page SEO?** *(mutiple answers)*

    A) They directly influence search engine rankings.

    B) They enhance the visual design of the website.

    C) They provide a brief summary that can improve click-through rates from search results.

    D) They automatically update to reflect the website's content.

    E) They offer enticing summaries that encourage users to click through to the website.

Your Answer:

SEO for Recruitment

12. **Which of the following describes the function of keyword optimisation in SEO?** *(mutiple answers)*

    A) It increases social media followers.

    B) It ensures content aligns with what users are searching for.

    C) It directly boosts the website's speed.

    D) It protects the website from hacking.

    E) It helps improve a website's relevance to search queries.

Your Answer:

---

13. **Which of the following statements about the role of technical SEO are true?** *(mutiple answers)*

    A) Technical SEO can enhance on-page SEO by creating a stronger foundation for t the website.

    B) Technical SEO includes keyword optimisation within website content.

    C) Technical SEO is primarily focused on external backlinks.

    D) Technical SEO improves the website's crawlability and indexing by search engines.

Your Answer:

---

14. **Which of these are goals of Technical SEO?** *(mutiple answers)*

    A) Improving website speed and performance

    B) Enhancing social media engagement metrics

    C) Optimising site structure for better crawling and indexing

    D) Securing connections between the website and its visitors

    E) Increasing email subscription rates

Your Answer:

SEO for Recruitment

15. **Which aspect of Technical SEO directly benefits on-page SEO by improving page load speed?** *(mutiple answers)*

   A) Comprehensive XML sitemaps

   B) Website speed optimisation

   C) Structured data markup

   D) Secure connections *(HTTPS)*

   E) Image optimisation

Your Answer:

16. **Which of the following are benefits of content quality?** *(mutiple answers)*

   A) It provides value to your audience, meeting their search intent.

   B) It helps engage visitors, encouraging them to spend more time on your website.

   C) It improves click-through rates by making your site more relevant in search results.

   D) It establishes your website's authority and trustworthiness.

   E) It enhances the overall user experience, leading to lower bounce rates.

Your Answer:

17. **Which elements of on-page SEO is primarily responsible for improving the structure and readability of content?** *(mutiple answers)*

   A) Meta descriptions

   B) Header tags *(H1, H2, etc.)*

   C) Internal linking

   D) Comprehensive XML sitemaps

   E) URL structure

Your Answer:

18. Which of the following statements about PPC advertising and organic SEO are true?

    A) PPC advertising directly improves organic SEO rankings.

    B) PPC advertising increases site visibility but does not directly boost organic SEO rankings.

    C) PPC advertising decreases organic SEO effectiveness by competing for the same keywords.

    D) PPC is a replacement for organic SEO efforts.

Your Answer:

19. What is the relationship between structured data markup and content visibility?

    A) Structured data markup allows for the use of larger text blocks.

    B) It increases page load speed.

    C) It helps search engines understand the content's context, potentially leading to rich snippets.

    D) It allows for more visual elements to be added.

Your Answer:

20. Which of the following statements about social media and SEO are false? (mutiple answers)

    A) Social media shares and likes are direct ranking factors in SEO.

    B) Social media has no impact on SEO at all.

    C) Social media can increase visibility and drive traffic, indirectly benefiting SEO.

    D) Social media directly improves organic SEO rankings.

Your Answer:

SEO for Recruitment

21. Which of the following is a key benefit of a comprehensive XML sitemap?

A) It lists all important pages for easier crawling by search engines.

B) It acts as a navigation aid for users.

C) It improves the website's design appeal.

D) It secures the website's data from cyber threats.

Your Answer:

22. How does on-page SEO complement off-page SEO?

A) On-page SEO directly reduces the need for backlinks.

B) On-page SEO builds the foundation for a website's content, while off-page SEO establishes its reputation and authority.

C) On-page SEO only focuses on content quality, while off-page SEO manages technical elements.

D) On-page SEO and off-page SEO are mutually exclusive.

Your Answer:

23. How does Off-Page SEO contribute to improving a website's overall reputation?
(mutiple answers)

A) By enhancing its crawlability for search engines.

B) By acquiring backlinks and brand mentions from reputable external sources.

C) By building relationships with influencers and partners to promote content.

D) By using relevant keywords in all marketing content.

E) By improving the site's credibility through external endorsements.

Your Answer:

24. How does regular technical SEO auditing contribute to overall SEO effectiveness?

   A) It increases the number of keywords used on each page.

   B) It ensures the website complies with international regulations.

   C) It identifies and rectifies SEO issues, maintaining optimal website performance.

   D) It enhances the visual design of the website.

Your Answer:

25. Why is the synergy between content layout and mobile responsiveness important for SEO?

   A) It ensures that content is always shown in landscape mode.

   B) It enables content to change dynamically.

   C) It restricts the amount of content on each page.

   D) It optimises content for all devices, enhancing usability and rankings.

Your Answer:

26. Why is it important to avoid "keyword stuffing" in SEO?

   A) Search engines penalise websites that overuse keywords, which can hurt rankings.

   B) Keyword stuffing improves rankings but decreases user experience.

   C) It leads to immediate penalties from search engines.

   D) It automatically removes content from search engine indexes.

Your Answer:

Test Answers

Introduction to SEO Correct Answers

1. B, 2. B, 3. B, 4. C, 5. B, 6. B, 7. C, 8. B

On-Page SEO Correct Answers

1. B, 2. B, 3. B, 4. B, 5. C, 6. B, 7. D, 8. B

Technical SEO Correct Answers

1. B, 2. C, 3. C, 4. C, 5. D, 6. B, 7. C, 8. C

Synergy, Myths and Misconceptions Correct Answers

1. B, 2. B, 3. D, 4. B, 5. B, 6. C, 7. B, 8. B

How Much Have You Learned Correct Answers

1. B & E, 2. B & D, 3. A, 4. E, 5. A & D, 6. B, 7. A, 8. B, 9. A, D & E, 10. A, B & D, 11. C & E, 12. B & E, 13. A & D, 14. A, C & D, 15. B & E, 16. A, B, C, D & E, 17. B & E, 18. B, 19. C, 20. A, B & D, 21. A, 22. B, 23. B, C & E, 24. C, 25. D, 26. A

Glossary

This glossary isn't an exhaustive list of every SEO term out there, but rather a collection of the key terms most relevant to this book. These are the concepts and definitions we've been asked about time and again—the terms that can often raise questions like, "What does this mean?" We've included clear, straightforward explanations to help you feel confident as you work through the material. Use this glossary as a quick reference guide whenever you need clarity on essential SEO vocabulary.

301

A 301 redirect is a permanent redirect from one URL to another. It is used to send both users and search engines to a different URL from the one they originally requested. The *"301"* status code indicates that the page has permanently moved to a new location. This type of redirect is particularly important in SEO because it helps maintain the inbound links or *"link juice"* and the associated SEO value of the original URL, transferring them to the new URL. It is commonly used when a website or a web page is moved to a new domain, or when URLs are changed for better organization or SEO. Implementing 301 redirects correctly is crucial for ensuring that users and search engines are directed to the correct pages and for preventing SEO issues related to duplicate content or broken links.

404

404 Error *(Not Found Error)* is a standard HTTP response code that indicates that the client was able to communicate with the server, but the server could not find the requested page. This error often occurs when a webpage has been deleted or moved without redirecting the old URL to a new page, or if the URL was typed incorrectly. For website visitors, encountering a 404 error can be a frustrating experience, as it interrupts their browsing activity. From an SEO perspective, too many 404 errors can negatively impact a site's usability and rankings because they disrupt the user experience and can harm the site's credibility with search engines. To manage 404 errors effectively, webmasters often create custom 404 error pages that guide users back to a working page on the site or to other useful resources, thereby improving the user experience and maintaining site engagement.

A/B Testing

A/B testing, also known as split testing, is the process of comparing two versions of a web page or app to see which one performs better. By showing the two variants to different segments of visitors at the same time, marketers can gather data on which version achieves higher conversion rates or better user engagement.

Alt Tags

Alt tags are attributes used in HTML and XHTML documents to specify alternative text that is to be displayed in place of an image if the image itself cannot be displayed. This text helps screen-reading tools describe images to visually impaired readers and allows search engines to better crawl and rank your website. Alt tags are also used to improve the SEO and usability of a site. They provide a textual alternative to images for search engines to index and help improve the relevance of search results by giving context to the images. In terms of SEO best practices, alt tags should be descriptive, specific, and contain any relevant keywords that accurately reflect the image content.

Anchor Text

Anchor text is the visible, clickable text in a hyperlink within digital content. It is significant in SEO because it provides context to both users and search engines about the content of the link's destination page. Optimising anchor text to include relevant keywords can enhance a site's relevance for those keywords, influencing its search rankings.

Audience

Customers + Prospects + Advocates = Audience. Obviously your customers are your focus but if you ignore the others your business will lose out. By *'advocates',* we mean employees, suppliers and partners. Your content must reach all these people so they act as you want them to: buy from you, supply to you, work for and with you, talk well of you.

Backlinks

Backlinks, also known as inbound links or incoming links, are links from one website to a page on another website. They are critical to SEO because search engines, especially Google, consider them as a significant ranking factor. Backlinks from high-quality and relevant websites are viewed as a vote of confidence that the content on the linked-to site is valuable and credible. This can positively impact the site's search engine ranking. The quality, quantity, and relevance of backlinks influence a website's domain authority and its visibility in search engine results pages *(SERPs)*. Effective backlink strategies can include guest blogging, creating shareable content, and engaging in partnerships, all aimed at generating more inbound links from reputable sources.

Black Hat SEO

Black Hat SEO refers to aggressive SEO strategies, techniques, and tactics that focus only on search engines and not a human audience, and usually does not obey search engines guidelines. Examples of black hat SEO techniques include keyword stuffing, invisible text, adding unrelated keywords to the page content, or page swapping.

Bounce Rate

Bounce rate is a metric that measures the percentage of visitors who enter a website and then leave *("bounce")* rather than continuing to view other pages within the same site. This metric is used to assess user engagement, with a high bounce rate often indicating that site entrance pages are not relevant or compelling to visitors. Bounce rates can vary significantly depending on the nature of a page: for instance, a high bounce rate on a contact information page might be normal, but it could indicate problems on a homepage or product page. Understanding bounce rates can help webmasters and marketers improve their website's user interface and content to better meet the needs of visitors, potentially increasing their engagement and the effectiveness of the site.

Brand

Your brand is you – everything you do, say and show. It's more than your logo and choice of colours. Whether you are posting on social media, talking to a customer over the phone or using another company to deliver a product, your brand is behind it all.

Canonical Tags

Canonical tags *(rel="canonical")* are HTML elements used to prevent duplicate content issues in SEO by specifying the *"canonical"* or *"preferred"* version of a web page. They are helpful when there are multiple similar pages with identical or highly similar content accessible via different URLs. By using the canonical tag, webmasters can tell search engines which version of a page to prioritize during indexing. This helps to concentrate all potential ranking power and link signals to one preferred URL, thereby avoiding potential search engine penalties for duplicate content and ensuring that the most relevant page is shown in search results. Canonical tags are essential for maintaining a clean and efficient website architecture, especially for large sites with many pages that could otherwise compete against each other in SERPs.

Communication

Basically, this is getting your content out there as copy and images, on your *'official'* publishing platforms *(eg website, social media channels, blogs)* as well as *'informal'* opportunities *(on the phone, networking, down the pub, etc)*. It also includes print and face-to-face presentations. Whether you are promoting, advertising, informing or educating, it's all regarded as communication.

Content

Content is your Brand Manual – an overarching guide to what you say, do and show. It's the sum total of your brand, no-one else's. *'Content'* is a loose term to describe words and images online. We also see it as a more inclusive concept that embraces everything about you and the people who matter to you. Then, what you write and show – online, in print and face-to-face – will portray a consistent brand whether you are detailing product features or outlining a solution to a customer's specific problem. Your content gives context to every word and image.

Content Management System *(CMS)*

A Content Management System *(CMS)* is software that helps users create, manage, and modify content on a website without the need for specialized technical knowledge. Popular CMS platforms like WordPress, Joomla, and Drupal enable non-technical users to build and manage websites efficiently.

Content Marketing

Content marketing is a strategic marketing approach focused on creating and distributing valuable, relevant, and consistent content to attract and retain a clearly-defined audience — and, ultimately, to drive profitable customer action. Unlike one-off advertising, content marketing shows that you understand and care about your customers' needs by providing them with information that helps them solve their challenges. It involves various formats, including blog posts, videos, podcasts, and social media content, aimed at building trust and relationships with potential and existing customers.

Conversion Funnel

A conversion funnel is a model that represents the stages a prospect goes through, from initial awareness of a brand or product to the final action or conversion. This model helps marketers understand and optimize the paths that users take to complete conversions, such as making a purchase or subscribing to a newsletter.

Conversion Rates

Conversion rates measure the percentage of visitors to a website who complete a desired action out of the total number of visitors. A *"conversion"* can include actions such as making a purchase, signing up for a newsletter, registering for a webinar, downloading a white paper, or any other measurable action that is valuable to the business. Conversion rates are a critical metric in digital marketing as they indicate the effectiveness of the website design, content, and user interface in persuading visitors to take the business's desired action. Higher conversion rates typically signify more efficient and effective user engagement and marketing strategies, directly impacting the profitability and success of online business activities.

Copywriting

The words you use to communicate your content. These words and how you use them *(style and tone)* must be appropriate to whom you're talking. You must also recognise that each channel requires a different approach. For example, a Facebook post is not the same as copy for a web page or a blog.

CTR

CTR or Click-Through Rate is a key performance metric in digital marketing that measures the ratio of users who click on a specific link to the number of total users who view a page, email, or advertisement. It is typically expressed as a percentage, calculated by dividing the number of clicks by the number of impressions *(views)* and multiplying the result by 100. In the context of SEO and pay-per-click *(PPC)* advertising, CTR is used to assess the effectiveness of online ads and search engine results. A higher CTR indicates that more people found the ad or search result relevant and enticing enough to click through to the website. For SEO, improving CTR can signal to search engines that a page is valuable to searchers, potentially boosting its rankings. For PPC, a higher CTR helps improve the ad's quality score, reducing cost per click and improving ad position.

Domain Authority

Domain Authority *(DA)* is a metric developed by Moz that predicts how well a website will rank on search engine result pages *(SERPs)*. It scores from 1 to 100, with higher scores corresponding to a greater likelihood of ranking. DA is calculated by evaluating multiple factors, including linking root domains and the number of total links, into a single DA score.

Engagement Rate

Engagement rate is a metric used to measure the level of interaction that users have with content on a website or social media platform. It is calculated by considering various factors such as the number of likes, shares, comments, or other interactions a piece of content receives relative to the number of users who see it or the number of followers the platform has. In the context of a website, engagement rate might also include metrics such as page views, time spent on site, or interactions with site elements like forms and buttons. This rate is an important indicator of how compelling and relevant users find the content, and it helps publishers and marketers understand the effectiveness of their content strategies in engaging their audience.

Google Analytics

Google Analytics is a free web analytics service offered by Google that tracks and reports website traffic. It is a powerful tool for marketers to understand how users find and use their website, providing insights that can help to optimise marketing campaigns, drive traffic, and improve retention and engagement.

Google Search Console

Google Search Console is a free web service offered by Google that helps website owners monitor, maintain, and troubleshoot their site's presence in Google Search results. It provides tools and reports that help you understand how Google views your site, allowing you to optimise your performance in search results. Key features include checking indexing status, submitting sitemaps, viewing traffic data, understanding keyword performance, and receiving alerts about issues that could affect your site's visibility, such as crawl errors or security issues.

Header Tags

Header Tags *(H1, H2, H3, etc.)* are HTML elements used to designate headings and subheadings within the content of a web page, differentiating them from paragraph text. These tags range from H1 to H6, representing different levels of headings; H1 is typically used for the main title of the page and is the most significant in terms of SEO impact, while H2 and lower represent various levels of subheadings. Proper use of header tags helps structure the content clearly for both users and search engines, enhancing readability and SEO. Header tags play a critical role in organising information on a page, making it easier for search engines to understand the hierarchy and major themes of the content, which can contribute to improved search engine rankings.

Heatmap

A heatmap is a visual tool used to represent where users click, scroll, or move within a webpage, showing areas of high and low activity. Heatmaps are valuable for understanding user behaviour on a site, which can help improve website design and user experience to increase effectiveness in achieving business goals.

HTTP

HTTP or Hypertext Transfer Protocol is the foundational protocol used for transmitting data over the web. It defines a method for communication between web browsers and servers, allowing users to fetch HTML pages, images, and other resources from web servers. HTTP operates as a request-response protocol in the client-server computing model, where web browsers request data from a server, which then responds with the requested information. Unlike HTTPS, HTTP does not encrypt its data, which can leave it vulnerable to interception by third parties. Due to this security concern, HTTPS, which encrypts data, is generally recommended for securing sensitive transactions.

HTTPS

HTTPS or Hypertext Transfer Protocol Secure is the secure version of HTTP, which is the primary protocol used to send data between a web browser and a website. HTTPS encrypts the communication between the browser and the website, enhancing security by protecting data from being intercepted, tampered with, or stolen by cyber attackers. This is achieved by using an SSL *(Secure Sockets Layer)* or TLS *(Transport Layer Security)* certificate, which secures the connection and ensures that any data transferred remains private and integral. HTTPS is crucial for protecting user-sensitive transactions, such as online banking and shopping, and is considered a standard web security practice. It is also a ranking factor in search engines, meaning websites using HTTPS are more likely to rank higher in search results.

Indexing

Indexing is the process by which search engines organize information before a search to enable fast responses to queries. When a web page is indexed by search engines, it is stored in a giant database from where it can be retrieved. Essentially, the process of indexing is identifying the words and expressions that best describe the page and assigning the page to particular keywords.

Internal Links

Internal links are hyperlinks that point to other pages or resources within the same domain. These are used to help navigate between pages on a website, providing a structured pathway for both users and search engines to access information. Internal linking is a crucial aspect of SEO because it helps to establish site architecture and spread link equity *(ranking power)* throughout the site. Effective internal linking can lead to better indexing by search engines as it makes it easier for search engine crawlers to find and index all pages of the site. For users, internal links improve the usability of a website by providing relevant additional information and suggesting other content of interest, which can enhance user engagement and reduce bounce rates.

IP Address

IP Address or Internet Protocol Address is a unique string of numbers separated by periods *(IPv4)* or colons *(IPv6)* that identifies each computer using the Internet Protocol to communicate over a network. IP addresses are essential for internet functionality as they ensure that data reaches the correct destination on a network. There are two types of IP addresses: IPv4, which consists of four groups of numbers from 0 to 255 *(e.g., 192.168.1.1)*, and IPv6, which is an alphanumeric address separated by colons designed to take over due to the limited number of available IPv4 addresses. In SEO, understanding IP addresses can be important, particularly when analyzing website traffic sources, managing site security, and determining the geographical distribution of visitors.

Keyword Research

Keyword research is the process of identifying and analysing terms that people use in search engines with the aim of using that data for a specific purpose, often for search engine optimization *(SEO)* or general marketing.

It involves understanding one's audience and how they seek out information online, determining the keywords relevant to your content or business, and gauging the demand and competition for these terms. This research helps inform content strategies and improve website visibility by targeting the phrases likely to attract the right visitors.

Keywords

Keywords are words or phrases that describe the content on your page or post best. They are the terms that searchers enter into search engines and are central to the field of search engine optimisation *(SEO)*. Keywords are essential because they inform search engines about the content of the webpage, and they help determine when and where your page will appear in search engine results pages *(SERPs)*. Effective keyword research and selection are crucial for SEO as they help match a website's content with what potential visitors are looking for. Keywords can be broadly categorized into two types: short-tail keywords, which are general and consist of one or two words, and long-tail keywords, which are more specific and usually made up of three or more words. The strategic use of keywords enables marketers to drive targeted traffic to their sites by optimizing their content for the most relevant and profitable queries.

Landing Page

A landing page is a standalone web page created specifically for a marketing or advertising campaign. It's where a visitor *"lands"* after they click on a link in an email, or ads from Google, Bing, YouTube, Facebook, Instagram, Twitter, or similar places on the web. Unlike web pages, which typically have many goals and encourage exploration, landing pages are designed with a single focus or goal, known as a call to action *(CTA)*.

Link Building

Link building is the practice of acquiring hyperlinks from other websites to your own. It's a critical component of off-page SEO, as search engines use these links as indicators of your site's credibility and authority. Effective link building can significantly improve your site's search engine ranking and overall visibility. Strategies include creating high-quality, link-worthy content, guest blogging on reputable sites, and forming partnerships with other relevant sites. The goal is to have other websites link back to yours, demonstrating to search engines the value and trustworthiness of your content.

Long-Tail Keywords

Long-tail keywords are phrases that are more specific and usually longer than more commonly used keywords. They are less competitive, often resulting in higher conversion rates as they cater to more precise user intent.

Marketing

We like to use this word when we mean the bigger picture. Traditionally, marketing is everything involved in getting you to market: price, logistics, targeting, type of product and service offering, promotion.

Marketing Communication

Because *'communication'* has IT connotations, *'marketing communication'* is the accepted term to mean communicating in order to promote and explain your business.

Meta Description

A meta description is a brief summary of a webpage's content that appears under the page title in search engine results pages *(SERPs)*. Typically around 155 to 160 characters long, this HTML attribute provides a clear and concise explanation of the page's contents, intended to attract the reader's interest and convince them to click through to the website. While meta descriptions themselves do not influence a page's ranking in search engines, they are crucial for improving click-through rates *(CTRs)*, as a well-crafted meta description can make a webpage stand out among search results and drive more traffic to the site.

Meta Title

The meta title, also known as the title tag, is an HTML element that specifies the title of a web page. This title is displayed on search engine results pages *(SERPs)* as the clickable headline for a given result and is crucial for SEO, usability, and social sharing. The meta title is a primary element that search engines use to determine the topic of a web page, and it is considered a significant factor in influencing a page's search engine ranking. Ideally, a meta title should be concise, include relevant keywords, and be unique to each page to accurately reflect the content and entice users to click through from the search results.

Mobile Optimisation

Mobile optimisation involves designing and formatting your website to ensure it looks good and functions properly across all mobile devices. This practice is crucial for providing a positive user experience, as it adapts the layout and content to fit smaller screens and touch-based interactions. With mobile-first indexing by search engines, mobile optimisation also influences SEO rankings significantly.

Nofollow Link

A nofollow link is an HTML attribute *(rel="nofollow")* used to instruct search engines that a hyperlink should not influence the ranking of the link's target in the search engine's index. It is used to prevent spam and to indicate to search engines that the webmaster does not vouch for the content of the linked page.

Off-Page SEO

Off-page SEO encompasses actions taken outside of your own website to impact your rankings within search engine results pages *(SERPs)*. It includes strategies to build a website's reputation and authority through external means. Key off-page SEO tactics involve link building *(acquiring high-quality backlinks from other sites)*, social media marketing, and brand mentions. The goal is to increase the site's credibility and trustworthiness in the eyes of search engines, thereby improving visibility and search ranking.

On-Page SEO

On-page SEO involves optimising web page content for search engines and users

Common on-page SEO practices include optimising title tags, content, internal links, and URLs to improve a site's visibility and ranking in search engine results pages *(SERPs)*. It focuses on making the site more accessible and valuable to visitors, ensuring the website communicates its topic and value clearly to search engines. This practice is key to driving relevant traffic and improving user engagement.

Organic Traffic

Organic traffic refers to visitors who land on your website as a result of unpaid *(organic)* search results. It is distinct from paid traffic, which results from paid ads. Organic traffic is considered highly valuable because it is targeted; users are visiting your website because something about your page listing—like the title, meta description, or URL—stood out in the search engine results page *(SERP)* compelling them to click through. This type of traffic is driven by effective SEO practices such as using relevant keywords, optimizing meta tags, and creating quality content that ranks well in search engines. Organic traffic is a key performance indicator in digital marketing, as it is a sustainable source of web visitors over time and typically indicates a high level of interest and engagement from the audience.

Outbound Links

Outbound links are links from a website to another external site. These links lead users away from the site and direct them to different domains. In the context of SEO, outbound links are important because they can signal to search engines the relevance and quality of the content on a page. When a website links to reputable and relevant external sites, it can help establish credibility and authority, potentially improving its own search engine rankings. However, excessive use of outbound links or linking to low-quality or irrelevant sites can have a detrimental effect. Therefore, it's important to use outbound links judiciously, ensuring they add value for the user and are relevant to the content.

Page Speed

Page speed refers to the amount of time a page needs to be completely loaded within a browser. This metric affects both user experience and SEO rankings as search engines prioritise websites that provide faster loading times. Faster pages lead to better engagement, higher conversions, and improved search engine ranking positions.

PPC

PPC or Pay-Per-Click is a digital advertising model used to direct traffic to websites, in which an advertiser pays a publisher *(typically a website owner or a network of websites)* when the ad is clicked. It is commonly associated with first-tier search engines *(such as Google Ads and Bing Ads)*. With search engines, advertisers typically bid on keyword phrases relevant to their target market and pay when ads *(text-based search ads or shopping ads)* are clicked. In essence, PPC is a way of buying visits to your site, rather than attempting to *"earn"* those visits organically. PPC can be highly effective for businesses wanting to generate immediate traffic and conversions, as it allows for precise targeting and real-time performance measurement.

Responsive

Responsive design refers to a web design approach aimed at crafting sites to provide an optimal viewing and interaction experience across a wide range of devices *(from desktop monitors to mobile phones)*. This design approach uses fluid grids, flexible images, and CSS media queries to adapt the layout of the website to the viewing environment. The goal is to ensure that the website is easy to read and navigate with a minimum of resizing, panning, and scrolling, regardless of the device used. Responsive design is essential for enhancing user experience and improving site usability. From an SEO perspective, it also plays a crucial role because search engines like Google prioritize mobile-friendly websites in their search results, particularly for searches done on mobile devices. Thus, implementing responsive design is key to improving a website's search engine rankings and overall reach.

Rich Snippets

Rich snippets are enhanced search results displayed by search engines that provide additional data about the content of a webpage. These snippets include more information than the standard title, URL, and meta description, often featuring elements such as star ratings, images, author details, product prices, or other relevant data that can help a user better understand what the page is about before clicking through. Rich snippets are generated from structured data markup embedded in a website's HTML. They are important for SEO as they can significantly increase the click-through rate *(CTR)* from search engine results pages by making the listings more attractive and informative to potential visitors. Rich snippets do not directly affect rankings but can enhance visibility and user engagement, indirectly benefiting SEO performance.

Robots.txt

Robots.txt is a text file webmasters create to instruct web robots *(typically search engine crawlers)* how to crawl pages on their website. The file is placed at the root of the website's directory structure and provides protocols to agents about which areas of the site they are allowed or disallowed from accessing. Robots.txt is crucial for controlling the traffic of web crawlers, which can help prevent overloading your site with requests and ensure that important content is indexed while private or non-essential content remains unindexed. While it's powerful for directing crawler traffic, it's important to note that Robots.txt does not enforce visitor or bot behavior but rather serves as a guideline. Moreover, improper use of Robots.txt can accidentally block search engines from indexing important content, negatively impacting the site's SEO performance.

Schema

Schema or Schema Markup, often referred to simply as Schema, is a code *(semantic vocabulary)* that you put on your website to help the search engines return more informative results for users. It acts as a framework or schema that provides search engines with a better understanding of the content on your web pages. This can include information about a person, place, thing, event, or business in a structured format. When implemented, schema markup can enhance the way a page displays in SERPs by enabling rich snippets, which are enhanced descriptions that appear below the title and URL in search results. Examples include ratings for recipes, prices for products, or events' dates. Schema markup helps search engines interpret the context of information on websites, thus improving the quality of search results and potentially increasing click-through rates.

Search Engines

Search engines are systems that search for and identify information on the web based on keywords entered by users. They work by crawling, indexing, and retrieving web pages to display them as search results in response to user queries. The most well-known search engines include Google, Bing, and Yahoo. These platforms use complex algorithms to rank the content found during the search process, aiming to present the most relevant, authoritative, and useful results to users. Search engines play a crucial role in digital marketing and SEO as they determine how content is discovered and ranked, influencing web traffic, visibility, and engagement.

Search Intent

Search intent, also known as user intent, is the purpose behind a user's query on a search engine. It refers to what the user is looking to achieve when they type a search term into a search engine. Understanding search intent is crucial for SEO as it helps content creators align their pages with the needs and expectations of their audience. There are typically four main types of search intent:

- **Informational Intent:** The user seeks information, such as answers to questions or more details on a topic.
- **Navigational Intent:** The user wants to visit a specific website or page.
- **Transactional Intent:** The user is looking to make a purchase or engage in another type of transaction.
- **Commercial Investigation:** The user is considering a purchase and wants to compare options or read reviews.

Optimising content to match the specific search intent of target keywords can greatly enhance a site's relevance and authority, thus improving its rankings and user engagement.

Semantic Search

Semantic search uses artificial intelligence to understand the searcher's intent and the contextual meaning of terms as they appear in the searchable dataspace, whether on the Web or within a closed system, to generate more relevant results. Google's search technology relies on semantic search principles.

SEO *(search engine optimisation)*

The very specific on and off page techniques used to find your audience, then influence them into taking the right action – visit, call, buy, share, etc.

SERPs

SERPs or Search Engine Results Pages are the pages displayed by search engines in response to a user's query. These pages list the results of the search, typically including both organic search results and paid advertisements. The content of SERPs can vary depending on the query and may include listings of web pages, images, videos, infographics, articles, research papers, and other types of content that the search engine finds relevant to the user's query. SERPs are critical for SEO as they directly influence how content is displayed and accessed by users. The design and layout of SERPs can also change based on factors such as the user's location, search history, and whether they are using a mobile device or desktop.

Social Proof

Social proof is a psychological phenomenon where people conform to the actions of others under the assumption that those actions are reflective of the correct behavior. In digital marketing, social proof can be leveraged to increase conversions by showcasing customer testimonials, reviews, and large social media followings.

SSL

SSL or Secure Sockets Layer is a security technology that establishes an encrypted link between a web server and a browser. This link ensures that all data passed between the web server and browsers remain private and integral. SSL is commonly used to secure credit card transactions, data transfer, and logins, and more recently is becoming the norm when securing browsing of social media sites. SSL works by using a cryptographic system that uses two keys to encrypt data: a public key known to everyone and a private key known only to the recipient of the message. Websites that use SSL will display *"HTTPS"* in their URLs, indicating that the connection is secure.

Technical SEO

Technical SEO refers to the process of optimising the infrastructure of a website to enable search engines to crawl and index its pages more effectively.

It focuses on improving site structure, ensuring mobile-friendliness, enhancing page speed, securing the site with HTTPS, and implementing structured data *(schema markup)*.

Technical SEO is foundational, aiming to improve user experience and support other SEO efforts, such as on-page and off-page strategies, by making sure the website meets the technical requirements of modern search engines for improved ranking and visibility.

Title Tag

A title tag is an HTML element that specifies the title of a web page. Title tags are displayed on search engine results pages *(SERPs)* as the clickable headline for a given result and are important for usability, SEO, and social sharing. The title of a page is a critical indicator for both the search engine and the user; it provides a concise preview of the content and is often used by search engines as a major ranking factor. An effective title tag should be accurate, descriptive, and concise, containing key phrases that target the page's content. Optimising the title tag involves balancing keyword inclusion with readability and relevance, helping to improve a website's search engine rankings and click-through rates.

TSL

TLS or Transport Layer Security is a cryptographic protocol designed to provide secure communication over a computer network. It is the successor to Secure Sockets Layer *(SSL)* and is more secure and efficient. TLS uses stronger encryption algorithms and has the ability to work on different ports and protocols. It provides privacy and data integrity between two communicating applications, such as a web server and a browser. TLS is used to secure web browsers, emails, messaging apps, and other types of data transfers. Like SSL, when a website uses TLS, the URL will begin with *"HTTPS"* instead of *"HTTP,"* indicating that the connection is secure and encrypted.

URL

URL or Uniform Resource Locator is the address of a specific webpage or file on the internet. It provides the means for accessing information hosted on the web and includes a protocol *(such as HTTP or HTTPS)*, the domain name *(or IP address)*, and often a path to a specific page or resource within a website. URLs are fundamental to navigating the web, as they specify the location of every piece of content that users may need to access online. In SEO, a well-structured URL that includes relevant keywords can enhance a site's searchability and improve its visibility in search engine results pages *(SERPs)*.

User Experience *(UX)*

User Experience *(UX)* in the context of websites refers to the overall experience a person has when interacting with a website, especially in terms of how easy or pleasing it is to use. UX plays a critical role in SEO as search engines increasingly prioritise sites that offer high-quality user experiences, including mobile-friendliness, intuitive navigation, and fast load times.

User Intent

User intent refers to the goal or expectation that an internet user has when typing a query into a search engine. Understanding user intent is crucial for creating content that satisfies user needs and for optimizing for SEO, as search engines strive to deliver results that match the intent behind users' searches.

White Hat SEO

White Hat SEO refers to the usage of optimisation strategies, techniques, and tactics that focus on a human audience opposed to search engines and completely follows search engine rules and policies. Examples include using keywords, back linking, link building to improve link popularity, and writing content for human readers.

XML Sitemap

An XML sitemap is a file that helps search engines understand your website while crawling it. It acts as a roadmap to tell search engines what content is available and how to reach it. This XML file lists the URLs for a site along with additional metadata about each URL *(when it was last updated, how often it changes, and how important it is relative to other URLs in the site)* so that search engines can more intelligently crawl the site. XML sitemaps are particularly useful for websites that have large archives, new websites with just a few external links to it, or websites which use rich media content. While not mandatory, having an XML sitemap can be crucial for SEO, especially in helping search engines discover and index new pages faster.

Index

We've kept the index as straightforward as possible, focusing on key words and terms rather than every variation of every word. This approach mirrors the simplicity of the SEO for Recruitment book itself. You'll find that many topics are woven throughout the chapters, reflecting the holistic nature of SEO. This means some subjects appear across multiple pages and sections, offering you a comprehensive view as you explore the material. Use this index as a quick guide to locate essential concepts and revisit important discussions as needed.

Index

Symbols

301 Redirects 127, 159, 162, 166, 167, 183, 200
404 Redirects 167

A

Accessible Forms 148
Algorithm 27, 33, 34, 59, 73, 85, 105, 118, 122, 128, 213, 216
Alt Text 109, 110, 113, 116, 144, 145, 146
  Alt Text 35
Anchor Text 104, 105, 107, 108, 113, 201
ARIA 96, 100, 104, 107, 144, 148, 200
Audience Alignment 115

B

Black Hat 202
Body Content 95
Broken Image 110
Broken Link 61, 63, 106, 107, 119, 158, 162, 200
Browser Caching 128, 129, 131
Browsers 116, 131, 154, 158, 173, 206, 215, 216

C

Call To Action 208
Canonical Tags 126, 165, 166, 183, 202, 203
CMS 134, 140, 141, 143, 153, 154, 159, 161, 162, 164, 177, 182, 184, 203
  CMS 114
CMS Integration 154
Content 2, 23, 26, 29, 30, 32, 33, 34, 35, 36, 37, 38, 39, 42, 43, 44, 46, 47, 48, 49, 50, 51, 52, 56, 58, 59, 61, 62, 63, 64, 66, 68, 69, 70, 72, 73, 74, 75, 76, 79, 80, 81, 84, 85, 86, 87, 88, 89, 90, 91, 92, 93, 94, 95, 96, 97, 98, 99, 105, 106, 107, 109, 110, 111, 112, 113, 114, 115, 116, 117, 118, 119, 120, 124, 125, 126, 131, 132, 133, 134, 135, 136, 137, 138, 140, 142, 144, 145, 146, 147, 148, 149, 150, 151, 152, 153, 154, 155, 156, 157, 158, 160, 161, 162, 165, 166, 167, 172, 174, 175, 176, 177, 183, 184, 187, 188, 189, 190, 191, 192, 193, 194, 195, 196, 197
Content Freshness 88, 114, 118
Content Management System 131, 134, 140, 203
  Content Management System 114
Content Quality 47, 87, 115, 194, 196
Conversion Rate 35, 46, 51, 69, 79, 128, 201, 204, 209
Core Web Vitals 136, 137, 170, 172, 173, 174
  Core Web Vitals 130
CPD 1
CSS 131, 142, 212
  CSS 128
CTA 88, 99, 113, 118, 122, 128, 159, 208, 214, 217
Cumulative Layout Shift 174, 175
  Cumulative Layout Shift 137
SSL 2, 35, 56, 59, 99, 104, 123, 126, 139, 140, 141, 142, 172, 181, 183, 184

D

Digital Marketing 3, 23, 26, 47, 204, 211, 213, 215
Domain Authority 202, 205
Duplicate Content 61, 75, 81, 98, 115, 161, 162, 165, 166, 190, 200, 202, 203

E

Engagement 28, 35, 39, 43, 47, 56, 60, 62, 69, 70, 85, 86, 87, 88, 120, 122, 124, 128, 170, 172, 190, 192, 193, 200, 201, 202, 204, 205, 207, 211, 212, 213, 214

F

First Input Delay 137, 174, 175
  First Input Delay 137

SEO for Recruitment

G

Google 33, 48, 61, 62, 73, 75, 76, 94, 105, 106, 111, 117, 118, 128, 129, 132, 133, 134, 135, 139, 143, 144, 150, 151, 152, 153, 154, 163, 164, 165, 172, 173, 176, 177, 178, 181, 184, 185, 201, 205, 208, 212, 213, 214
Google Analytics 129, 173, 205
   Google Analytics 129
Google Search Console 106, 143, 154, 164, 165, 181, 184, 185, 205

H

Headers 43, 47, 48, 84, 89, 90, 91, 92, 94, 95, 111, 112, 113, 115, 116, 186
   Headers 35
Headings 48, 90, 91, 92, 93, 113, 145, 147, 206
HTML 35, 38, 42, 47, 107, 135, 137, 153, 166, 175, 201, 202, 206, 209, 210, 212, 216
HTTP 57, 61, 62, 69, 74, 75, 79, 80, 123, 139, 140, 141, 142, 143, 166, 171, 172, 180, 181, 182, 183, 184, 185, 186, 190, 194
HTTPS 57, 61, 62, 69, 74, 75, 79, 80, 123, 139, 140, 141, 142, 143, 166, 171, 172, 180, 181, 182, 183, 184, 185, 186, 190, 194, 206, 207, 215, 216
   HTTPS 57

I

Image Optimisation 48, 52, 69, 76, 80, 86, 109, 113, 116, 194
   Image Optimisation 43
Indexation 125, 126, 163, 164
   Indexation 125
Internal Linking 43, 48, 52, 53, 70, 104, 105, 113, 190, 191, 194, 207

J

Javascript 131, 137, 175
   Javascript 128

K

Keyword Density 94
Keyword Optimisation 35, 43, 47, 52, 70, 116, 186, 189, 190, 193
Keyword Placement 85, 89, 93
Keyword Research 29, 30, 33, 37, 93, 94, 96, 112, 113, 119, 208
Keywords 29, 30, 32, 34, 35, 38, 42, 43, 47, 48, 70, 72, 75, 78, 80, 81, 85, 86, 89, 90, 91, 93, 94, 95, 96, 99, 101, 107, 108, 110, 112, 113, 116, 119, 126, 147, 156, 157, 158, 160, 186, 190, 191, 192, 195, 196, 197, 201, 202, 207, 208, 209, 210, 211, 213, 214, 216, 217
Keyword Stuffing 72, 80, 94, 95, 197, 202

L

Largest Contentful Paint 136
Largest Contentful Paint (LCP) 174
Largest Contentful Paint (LPC) 174
Lazy Loading 110, 129, 131, 137, 174, 178
Link Building 28, 31, 35, 39, 89, 191, 209, 210, 217
Link Labelling 104
Load Time 38, 53, 79, 86, 109, 110, 126, 129, 130, 131, 172, 217

M

Meta Description 43, 47, 51, 52, 74, 78, 85, 86, 94, 95, 97, 98, 99, 100, 111, 114, 190, 192, 194
Meta Descriptions 43, 47, 51, 52, 78, 85, 86, 97, 98, 114, 190, 192, 194, 209
Meta Title 179
Meta Titles 179
Misconceptions 65, 66, 67, 72, 78, 198
Mobile-Friendly 52, 117, 126, 132, 133, 134, 135, 171, 172, 176, 177, 178, 212
   Mobile-Friendly 48
Multimedia 112, 113, 119, 135, 145, 149
Myths 65, 66, 67, 72, 198

N

Navigation 53, 63, 78, 80, 86, 104, 105, 123, 124, 125, 134, 135, 136, 144, 145, 146, 147, 156, 157, 158, 160, 177, 191, 196
Nofollow 106, 210

O

Off-page SEO 30
Off-Page SEO 27, 28, 30, 35, 36, 38, 39, 186, 189, 191, 196, 209, 210
On-page SEO 30
   On-Page SEO 30
On-Page SEO 30, 31, 35, 36, 38, 39, 41, 42, 43, 44, 45, 46, 47, 48, 49, 50, 51, 52, 53, 66, 68, 69, 70, 71, 79, 80, 83, 84, 85, 88, 89, 90, 176, 189, 192, 193, 194, 196, 198, 210, 211
   On-Page SEO 30
On-Page SEO Test 43
Optimisation 32, 33, 34, 35, 39, 43, 45, 47, 48, 52, 56, 57, 58, 59, 60, 66, 67, 69, 70, 76, 78, 80, 86, 93, 108, 109, 113, 114, 116, 117, 123, 126, 128, 129, 130, 132, 133, 134, 171, 172, 186, 187, 189, 190, 193, 194, 208, 210, 214, 217
Organic Rankings 76
Organic Search 46, 77, 172
Organic Traffic 44, 46, 191, 211
Outbound Link 86, 104, 105, 107, 211

P

Page Experience 170, 171, 172, 173
Pagespeed Insights 129
   Pagespeed Insights 128

Plugins *131, 140, 141, 150, 153, 154, 182*
Primary Keyword *48, 94, 95, 96, 98, 157*
Primary Keywords *94, 114*

R

Ranking *27, 28, 30, 33, 35, 36, 39, 42, 43, 44, 45, 46, 47, 48, 51, 58, 59, 60, 61, 62, 66, 68, 72, 73, 74, 75, 76, 77, 79, 81, 84, 85, 86, 87, 88, 89, 94, 109, 118, 122, 123, 124, 125, 126, 128, 133, 139, 170, 171, 172, 173, 176, 180, 186, 190, 191, 192, 195, 197, 200, 201, 203, 205, 206, 207, 209, 210, 211, 212, 214, 215, 216*
Redirecting *142, 159*
Redirection *166*
   Redirection 162
Responsive Web Design *133, 134, 177*
   Responsive Web Design 133
Rich Snippets *69, 80, 150, 190, 195, 212, 213*
   Rich Snippets 69
Robots.txt *57, 59, 126, 163, 164, 213*

S

Schema *124, 126, 150, 151, 152, 153, 154, 155, 213, 215*
   Schema 124
Search *23, 26, 27, 28, 29, 30, 31, 32, 33, 34, 35, 36, 37, 38, 39, 42, 43, 44, 45, 46, 47, 48, 49, 50, 51, 52, 53, 56, 57, 58, 59, 60, 61, 62, 63, 64, 66, 67, 69, 70, 72, 73, 74, 75, 76, 77, 80, 81, 84, 85, 86, 87, 88, 89, 90, 93, 94, 95, 96, 97, 98, 99, 104, 105, 106, 108, 109, 110, 111, 112, 113, 114, 115, 116, 118, 119, 122, 123, 124, 125, 126, 128, 139, 140, 142, 143, 144, 150, 151, 153, 154, 156, 157, 158, 160, 161, 163, 164, 165, 170, 171, 172, 176, 179, 180, 181, 184, 185, 186, 187, 189, 190, 191, 192, 193, 194, 195, 196, 197, 200, 201, 202, 203, 204, 205, 206, 207, 208, 209, 210, 211, 212, 213, 214, 215, 216, 217*
Search Intent *30, 47, 75, 111, 115, 189, 194, 214*
Secure Browsing *59, 60*
SEO *1, 2, 3, 21, 22, 23, 25, 26, 27, 28, 29, 30, 31, 32, 33, 34, 35, 36, 37, 38, 39, 41, 42, 43, 44, 45, 46, 47, 48, 49, 50, 51, 52, 53, 55, 56, 57, 58, 59, 60, 61, 62, 63, 64, 66, 67, 68, 69, 70, 71, 72, 73, 74, 75, 76, 77, 78, 79, 80, 81, 83, 84, 85, 86, 87, 88, 89, 90, 93, 94, 96, 104, 105, 108, 109, 111, 112, 113, 119, 121, 122, 123, 124, 125, 126, 127, 128, 130, 133, 139, 144, 145, 150, 154, 156, 157, 158, 160, 162, 163, 170, 171, 172, 173, 176, 179, 180, 181, 186, 187, 188, 189, 190, 191, 192, 193, 194, 195, 196, 197, 198, 200, 201, 202, 204, 205, 206, 207, 208, 209, 210, 211, 212, 213, 214, 215, 216, 217*
SERPs *33, 35, 44, 45, 58, 59, 61, 64, 93, 124, 179, 202, 203, 205, 208, 209, 210, 211, 213, 214, 215, 216*
Site Hierarchy *156, 158*
SSL Certificate *139, 140, 141, 142, 172, 181, 183*
   SSL Certificate 139

T

Technical SEO *31, 38, 47, 48, 49, 54, 55, 56, 57, 58, 59, 60, 62, 63, 64, 68, 69, 70, 78, 79, 121, 122, 123, 124, 125, 126, 128, 133, 144, 150, 156, 170, 171, 172, 186, 189, 190, 191, 192, 193, 194, 197, 198, 215*
Title Tags *47, 74, 78, 85, 86, 97, 98, 211, 216*
   Title Tags 43
TLS Certificate *183, 184*

U

URL *43, 47, 48, 52, 61, 64, 70, 80, 96, 115, 124, 125, 126, 129, 135, 142, 143, 153, 154, 156, 157, 158, 159, 160, 161, 162, 163, 165, 166, 167, 178, 179, 183, 184, 186, 190, 194, 200, 202, 203, 211, 212, 213, 215, 216, 217*
URL Structure *48, 52, 70, 96, 124, 125, 126, 156, 157, 159, 160, 161, 190, 194*
   URL Structure 43
User Experience *32, 35, 43, 46, 47, 48, 51, 57, 59, 60, 61, 68, 69, 73, 76, 78, 84, 86, 87, 96, 104, 107, 109, 110, 115, 122, 123, 124, 127, 128, 136, 140, 144, 156, 157, 166, 171, 173, 174, 176, 194, 197, 200, 206, 210, 211, 212, 215, 216, 217*
User Intent *46, 111, 115, 209, 214, 217*

V

Value Proposition *96, 115*

W

WCAG *145, 146*
WCAG Levels *146*
Web Content Accesibility Guidelines *145*
Web Page *29, 43, 44, 47, 52, 97, 163, 172, 200, 202, 204, 206, 207, 208, 210, 213, 214, 216*
Website *2, 3, 21, 22, 23, 27, 29, 30, 31, 32, 33, 34, 35, 36, 37, 38, 39, 42, 43, 44, 45, 46, 47, 48, 49, 51, 52, 53, 56, 57, 58, 59, 60, 61, 62, 63, 64, 66, 68, 69, 72, 73, 74, 75, 76, 78, 79, 80, 81, 84, 85, 86, 88, 89, 97, 104, 105, 106, 109, 111, 114, 118, 122, 123, 125, 126, 127, 128, 129, 130, 131, 133, 134, 135, 136, 137, 139, 140, 141, 142, 143, 144, 145, 146, 147, 149, 150, 151, 152, 156, 157, 158, 159, 161, 162, 164, 165, 166, 171, 172, 173, 174, 175, 176, 177, 178, 179, 180, 181, 182, 183, 184, 186, 187, 189, 190, 191, 192, 193, 194, 196, 197, 200, 201, 202, 203, 204, 205, 206, 207, 208, 209, 210, 211, 212, 213, 214, 215, 216, 217*
Website Speed *57, 60, 64, 78, 122, 126, 128, 129, 130, 193, 194*
   Website Speed 57
White Hat *76, 217*

X

XML *61, 63, 126, 140, 145, 164, 165, 181, 194, 196, 217*
XML Sitemap *61, 63, 126, 140, 145, 164, 165, 181, 194, 196, 217*

Enhance Your SEO Journey with
seo-training-online.co.uk

Explore our website at **seo-training-online.co.uk** to discover a range of resources designed to help you master SEO at your own pace. We offer a variety of training options, including online courses, interactive webinars, and personalised 1-2-1 business training packages. Our growing collection of books—available as standalone resources or as hard-copy companions to our courses—provides additional insights and support for your learning journey.

Our courses and materials are crafted to suit all experience levels, from beginners to seasoned professionals. With years of experience working across diverse industry sectors, we've tailored our offerings to meet specific industry needs. Our list of courses and books is always expanding, so if you don't see your industry represented, please reach out through our website. We may already have something in development, or we can discuss creating a bespoke course that fits your needs.

Visit us today and see how seo-training-online.co.uk can support you in achieving greater online visibility and success.

www.ingramcontent.com/pod-product-compliance
Lightning Source LLC
Chambersburg PA
CBHW071021240526
45469CB00006BD/2021